The Little Black Book of

BIG
RED
FLAGS

The Little Black Book of BIG RED FLAGS

Relationship Warning Signs
You Totally Spotted . . .
But Chose to Ignore

Natasha Burton, Julie Fishman, and **Meagan McCrary**
Founders of BigRedFlags.com

Avon, Massachusetts

Published by
Adams Media, a division of F+W Media, Inc.
57 Littlefield Street, Avon, MA 02322. U.S.A.
www.adamsmedia.com

ISBN 10: 1-4405-1265-5
ISBN 13: 978-1-4405-1265-0
eISBN 10: 1-4405-2486-6
eISBN 13: 978-1-4405-2486-8

Printed in the United States of America.

10   9   8   7   6   5   4   3   2   1

Library of Congress Cataloging-in-Publication Data
Burton, Natasha.
The little black book of big red flags / Natasha Burton, Julie Fishman, and Meagan McCrary.
p. cm.
ISBN-13: 978-1-4405-1265-0
ISBN-10: 1-4405-1265-5
ISBN-13: 978-1-4405-2486-8 (ebk)
ISBN-10: 1-4405-2486-6 (ebk)
1. Man-woman relationships. 2. Couples—Psychology. 3. Mate selection. I. Fishman, Julie.
II. McCrary, Meagan. III. Title.
HQ801.B8843 2011
646.7′7—dc22
2011008862

This publication is designed to provide accurate and authoritative information with regard to
the subject matter covered. It is sold with the understanding that the publisher is not engaged
in rendering legal, accounting, or other professional advice. If legal advice or other expert
assistance is required, the services of a competent professional person should be sought.
    —From a *Declaration of Principles* jointly adopted by a Committee of the American
              Bar Association and a Committee of Publishers and Associations

Many of the designations used by manufacturers and sellers to distinguish their product
are claimed as trademarks. Where those designations appear in this book and Adams
Media was aware of a trademark claim, the designations have been printed with initial
capital letters.

This book is available at quantity discounts for bulk purchases.
For information, please call 1-800-289-0963.

Dedication

Without the red-flag–ridden bad dates, lame hook-ups, and terrible boyfriends we've encountered, this book would not exist. So, thank you. We knew you'd be good for something, someday.

Red Flag (noun):

1. A sign of danger.

2. The point in time when you notice something is a tad off with the guy you're dating, but decide to let it go because you really like him, you're tired of being single, you really really want to get laid, whatever. Then, when things start going downhill, you look back on that seemingly insignificant moment you dismissed and think: *That's when I should have known.*

Contents

Acknowledgments

We'd like to thank our agent, Elizabeth Evans, for believing in us and in this book, as well as Brendan O'Neill, Wendy Simard, and the rest of the Adams Media team for their guidance throughout the publishing process.

To our loyal readers and fans of our blog: This book wouldn't exist without you. And we certainly couldn't have written it without inspiration from those of you who submitted your red-flag stories. Thank you for sharing your often hilarious and all-to-familiar tales with us.

We are also eternally grateful for our parents, grandparents, and siblings. And we could never have gotten this far without our amazing friends, who submitted stories to our blog (or didn't get mad when we posted them ourselves). Special thanks to Dave Holop, Greg St. Clair, Kathleen Carter, Lorena O'Neil, Scott Newman, and, last but not least, Justin Vesci, our number one fan and hands-down funniest blog commenter, who was there cheering us on from the beginning.

Introduction

Salute the Flag

No matter how preoccupied we are with crafting well-phrased Facebook statuses (Natasha), searching for the best food truck in Los Angeles (Julie), or interpreting astrological charts (Meagan), as three twenty-something female friends, we still find ourselves talking about boys. A lot.

While our dating styles and current relationship statuses are totally different—serial monogamist Natasha is coupled, habitually love-struck Meagan is single, and former fling fan Julie is married—as we've swapped stories of male conquests past and present over the course of our friendship, including tales of those who'd captured our hearts and subsequently squashed them, we found that most of our anecdotes lead back to one essential question: What the heck were we thinking? We can't believe the number of downright dreadful dudes we've encountered, how many Big Red Flags these men presented, and how completely insensible we were at certain points during our romantic careers.

Turns out that our men-related mishaps were not only hysterical in hindsight—no matter how terrible they seemed at the moment—they also offered us valuable lessons on what *not* to look for in a boyfriend. Reasoning that many women had similarly dicey dating pasts, and relationship horror stories of their own that needed to be shared, we created a website called *The Little Black Blog of Big Red Flags*. Starting with our own stories—and, trust us, we have a lot—the site grew quickly, and daily submissions came in from across the country and eventually from around the globe.

Soon our readers began sending in questions along with their dating tales, seeking advice from us on how to handle their particular red-flag situations. After rifling through thousands of submissions in order to find the most common red-flag moves carried out by dudes, we compiled these can't-believe-it-really-happened tales of dating disaster, along with our advice on how to handle them.

In the pages that follow, we'll be pointing out the red-flag–worthy problems men put out there, so you can evaluate what you're okay with, and what you're so not okay with, to gain a better understanding of what you want out of a partner and your relationship.

Keep in mind that a red flag isn't always a must-get-out-now offense (some are just good to know), and this book isn't intended to guy bash. Superficial complaints or personal pet peeves do not count as red flags. If you're expecting a guy to be perfect in every way and to never get on your nerves—ever—you're going to be waiting around a long time . . . and will most likely end up bitter and lonely, drinking boxed wine by yourself. While you shouldn't settle for a dude who doesn't treat you the way you deserve, you might want to reconsider some of your dating criteria if a man's bank account or ability to play a mean air guitar is your top priority.

On the other hand, if a man physically harms or threatens you, his behavior is a full-on deal breaker. You don't need this book, you need a restraining order. Like yesterday.

Because we are not psychologists, cops, or crisis-management professionals, we won't be covering abusive red flags.

How to Use This Book

You can go about reading this book however you like: traditionally from front to back or skipping around from chapter to chapter. Each of this book's five parts breaks down the most common red flags we've encountered, personally in some cases, but mainly through story submissions on our blog. In addition to these anecdotes (which have been edited for clarity and to protect anonymity), you'll find our advice for handling each flagtastic fiasco.

Throughout the book you'll also find the following features:

Red-Flag Rules: These are our general tenets to live by when dating and mating. Lovingly sprinkled within the chapters, they are also listed at the back of the book for whenever you need a quick refresher course in red-flag behavior.

WTF?: The most outrageous stories we've received from the blog's Red Flag Hall of Fame, these must-share tales are loosely linked to red-flag stories and the associated advice.

Top Ten Red Flags: After each chapter, you'll find a short list of crazy, creepy, or atrocious flags to file away for future reference.

Red-Flag Case Studies: Between each section you'll find these dissections of longer stories riddled with several red flags. See how many you can spot based on what you've learned from the preceding chapters.

Finding a guy to hold on to is often a trial-and-error process, during which you're bound to encounter more than a few flags. The point is to get better at spotting them and removing yourself from a situation that doesn't suit you. We've all either blatantly ignored or completely missed red flags, especially when we've fallen madly in love with a guy. If we didn't, there'd be no need for this book. Fumbling from time to time by dating a few Mr. Wrongs allows you to learn what makes you happy or miserable in a relationship, which will ultimately help you score a true-love touchdown.

So, read on to learn a little, laugh a lot, and improve your dating dexterity so you don't get stuck in a Big Red-Flag situation. After all, if you pay attention, no one can say "I told you so."

Part One

He's Not Really Your Boyfriend

Chapter One

He Doesn't Consider You His Girlfriend

So, you're kinda sorta seeing this guy, the two of you are "hooking up" (whatever that means), but you've never been more confused about where you stand . . . or lay.

We've learned this lesson the hard way: Just because you're sleeping with a guy, going out to dinner, receiving flowers from him on your birthday, and spending the night at his place every weekend, you're not necessarily his girlfriend unless you've had "the talk."

> *Red-Flag Rule #1:* If you're not sure whether or not you're a guy's girlfriend, you probably aren't.

Most men will try to avoid Defining The Relationship (which our guy friends refer to in shorthand as "DTR") as long as possible. If they never have that talk, they theoretically don't have to walk the walk. Until your relationship is defined, the guy in question has the green light to roll up on chicks and hit on them, by technicality alone.

Men get away with this behavior, too—because we let them. Either we buy into the idea that the dude should always be the one to take the lead and initiate some kind of "what are we?"

discussion or we're too chicken to ask. It's totally normal to fear rejection—sometimes not knowing is a lot more bearable than hearing "no." And, sure, by not bringing it up, you'll be able to stay in your whatever-this-is state longer. But, as any gal who's been in relationship purgatory can attest, the confusion can cause more anxiety than a missed period.

If discussing your status with your spit-swapping stallion sounds more daunting than filing your taxes, here are some ways he'll show you that you're not his girlfriend.

You're not his plus one.

The two of you enjoy each other's company as well as your independence, so it doesn't seem like a big deal when your guy goes on a snowboarding trip with his buddies and doesn't invite you. But when he's tagging along on a couples weekend getaway and doesn't mention anything about you joining, you might start to wonder whether his pals even know you exist.

Dudes in committed relationships want to bring their lady loves to functions with their family and friends, not only to announce they've found someone special but also to share significant holidays, birthdays, and vacations with the woman in their life. In fact, most adults expect a guy to bring his significant other to important get-togethers. If you're not his routine "plus one," it's a definite indication that you're not his girlfriend.

While this realization may sting, it provides the perfect opportunity to have a little DTR powwow. Tell him you want to be his social steady, not his girl on the side. A man who won't make you his plus one should be subtracted from your love life.

BIG RED-FLAG STORY:

"My boyfriend was good friends with a forty-something Hollywood debutante, who always invited him to red-carpet events and VIP parties. He was basically her plus one for everything. However, not once did he ask his friend to get my name on a list so that the three of us could enjoy the limelight. He was having a ball rubbing elbows with the rich and famous and didn't give a damn that I was sitting at home in my pajamas. I had to draw the line when they bought tickets to a Justin Timberlake concert and didn't ask me if I wanted to go too."

He treats you like a friend, not a flame.

Men are able to distinguish having sex from having a relationship, two things women usually put hand-in-hand. So, though you may be doing the deed with a certain fella, he may think you're just a pal who wears panties rather than a potential girlfriend. When you try to act like a "guy's girl" you run the risk of being treated like "one of the guys."

A bloke who offers sweet nothings in the bedroom but only fist bumps when outside it doesn't see you as a girlfriend, but a girl who's willing to sleep with him. Men haven't evolved that far from animals—if you're his girlfriend, he'll want to mark his territory. While he may be against full-blown PDA, there are less overt ways he can show affection, like squeezing your hand for a brief moment, rubbing your back, or moving his chair a little closer to yours.

Standoffish behavior indicates that he doesn't want people to think the two of you are an item, and doesn't want you to think you're anything more than a fuck buddy. Though his nonchalance may just irk you in the beginning, it'll slowly sap your spirit, especially if you've spent serious time between his sheets.

BIG RED-FLAG STORY:

"I was dating a guy in grad school who would pretty much ignore me in the class we had together. He acted like we barely knew each other even though we'd been sleeping together on the weekends since the start of the semester. At the end of every class, the students would gather to say goodbye. My guy would slap everyone five on his way out . . . including me . . . the girl he was going to screw later that night. When I finally called him out on it, he gave the excuse that I was 'too much of a distraction.'"

He flirts with other women.

Some men are bold enough to flirt with another woman right in front of you and still expect you to go home with them at the end of the night. It doesn't matter whether a chick approaches your so-called beau first, or he actively seeks her out, if he makes a pass at another lass, you best be believing you're not his lady. We don't care if the other woman is your friend from out of town, your underage sister, or the loneliest girl at the party—there's no excuse for your man to make eyes at anyone other than you.

> *Red-Flag Rule #2:* If he still claims to be "Single" on Facebook or hasn't deleted his Match.com profile, he's still actively looking for a girlfriend, which you apparently are not.

Natasha once dated a dude who would flirt with her roommate: asking to see her D-cup breasts, making suggestive jokes, and inviting her along on would-be private dates. She didn't hit her limit until one night at 2 a.m., while lying in his bed (after sex) he mentioned they should drive back to her place—a cool thirty-minute trek—because he "felt bad" that her roommate was "all alone." He then tried to justify this by claiming that he thought her roommate had a thing for him. (Can we say delusional?) Needless to say, if he's thinking about other women, or coming on to them in front of you, he's not your boyfriend.

BIG RED-FLAG STORY:

"After about a month of seeing this man (and I say man because he was forty-two), I invited him to my housewarming party. It was the first time he would be at my apartment and meet my friends. He arrived that night with a nice bottle of white wine, and I started giving him a tour of my place. Then, my former neighbor (an ex-stripper from Vegas with huge fake breasts) walked in—and the evening unraveled rapidly from there.

"Apparently, my boyfriend and this woman (who regularly slept with at least two guys a weekend) already knew each other, and as they shook hands the sexual undertones were deafening. This man, who I was going to dinners and movies with, as well as having sex with, did not speak to me the entire evening. No exaggeration. He conversed with no one all night—except, of course, my ex-neighbor with the massive porn star tits. They were inseparable until she left the party, at which point he said he was going to leave, too."

He's only available when it's convenient for him.

When you're the only one initiating rendezvous between you and your man, think about whether he wants to spend time with you because he likes you or because it's convenient and he has nothing else to do. If your guy blows you off or frequently "forgets" your plans to hang out, he may consider you a backup plan rather than a first choice. Likewise, a guy who won't commit to dinner until twenty minutes before he's supposed to pick you up is clearly waiting to make sure he's not going to miss out on whatever his buddies are doing.

In addition to making you feel trivial, this guy is undependable—he'll be around on sunny days but as soon as the clouds roll in, he'll run for cover, leaving you out to drown in the downpour. If he suddenly reappears the second the storm passes, you can assume he is a man of convenience, not commitment. A relationship isn't about being there when it's opportune, but more so when it's not. Any dude will show up for the party; a good dude will stay after to help you clean up.

BIG RED-FLAG STORY:

"On my way to meet this guy I'd been seeing at a concert, I stopped to get gas a couple of blocks away from the venue. When I tried to turn my car back on I discovered that the battery had died. After calling AAA, I texted the guy I was meeting to let him know what was going on. His response was super sweet at first: He asked if there was anything he could do, if I wanted him to meet me, etc. I told him where I was—right around the corner—and that I was waiting alone. No text back. I tried calling. No answer. Forty-five minutes later, AAA came, jumped my car, and I was on my way. I texted the guy to tell him that I was up and running again, and he called me back right away. Of course, he could hear his phone and answer my texts the minute I no longer needed his help, and, of course, he still wanted me to meet him at the concert . . . so he could get laid later."

He tells you he doesn't want a girlfriend.

When pressed to answer questions about the status of their relationship, many men respond with an "I told myself I" statement, like "I told myself I was going to be more selfish/would focus on my music/would put my career first/wouldn't have a girlfriend in grad school." All this information is useful on date three, but not something you should learn on date thirty-three.

> *Red-Flag Rule #3:* If you ask the guy you've been sleeping with where he sees the relationship going, and he replies, "I don't want us to be anything more than this," no matter how great the sex is, don't expect a commitment anytime soon.

Then there are men who announce that they're not—repeat not— interested in having a girlfriend, but we're too buzzed and busy flirting at the time to even register this flag on our radar. Or maybe we completely hear what the guy's saying but are convinced we'll be the one to change his mind—hey, at least we've got confidence!

Once a guy has openly declared his commitment to remaining single, it doesn't matter if you keep tampons at his house or spend every Saturday night cuddling and watching *I Love Lucy* reruns. He may act like a boyfriend and talk like a boyfriend, but unless he tells you he's changed his mind about being coupled, don't convince yourself that you're his girlfriend.

These upfront fellas won't hesitate to pull the "I-told-you-I-didn't-want-a-girlfriend" card the moment you have a complaint about anything relationship-related. Our unanimous advice on this one: Don't date a dude who point blank tells you he's not looking for a relationship.

BIG RED-FLAG STORY:

"I can't remember where exactly I met this guy, but I do remember him telling me pretty early on that since he was a pilot in the Air Force reserves he could be deployed to Iraq within however many months, and that he wasn't in the position for a relationship. Well, I must have heard 'pilot' and forgot the rest because soon after we were talking on the phone nightly, seeing each other every weekend, and starting to have sleepovers on weeknights. Then all of a sudden I didn't hear from him for three or four days. A little worried, the next time I saw him I asked him where he was and what had he been doing. Apparently, I had overstepped some sort of boundary because he very coldly told me that it wasn't any of my business, that I wasn't his girlfriend, and that he had told me he didn't want a relationship. That time I heard every word."

WTF? *"We took a shower together. I went down on him. When I stood up, he decided it was the opportune moment to tell me he was not looking for a relationship. Time to exit ASAP (as gracefully as possible)."*

THE BOTTOM LINE:
You may think you're in love with your charming chap simply because you get those giddy butterflies in your belly every time he comes around. But those flutters could be the work of anxious moths signaling that you're uneasy over not knowing how the guy really feels about you.

If you and your man aren't on the same page, recognize that despite any connection you think you have, the two of you won't work if he wants a hookup and you want a boyfriend: You'll merely end up feeling mistreated and unappreciated. Relationships are just as much about shared expectations and timing as they are about shared passion.

There's nothing worse than wondering whether or not you are—or are going to be—someone's girlfriend. In addition to confusion, an undefined relationship will remain static. You're just wasting your time sitting in limbo when you could ditch the noncommittal dude for a guy who'd be happy to call you his one-and-only.

And not to get all Carrie Bradshaw on you here, but we can't help but ask: When did it becomes less awkward to writhe naked on top of a guy than to ask him how he feels about you? If you're willing to go that far, you should be willing to ask him if he's your boyfriend.

TOP TEN RED FLAGS:
Real Pick-up Lines from Our Blog

1. "It's the end of the night and you obviously don't have any other options."
2. "I'm black from the waist down."
3. "I'm on the top of the hotness tree."
4. "You could be my girlfriend if you were twenty pounds skinnier."
5. "I may not be the best looking guy here, but I'm the only one talking to you."
6. "Just so you know, I have no problem banging sluts."
7. "You should come home with me: I go down on girls for hours."
8. "I don't want to date you. I just want to put my face in your tits."
9. "Can I confess something? I think you're going to be my wife."
10. "You're going to look a lot better in a few hours, so come find me then."

Chapter Two

He Treats You Like a Slut

No woman, regardless of her bedroom behavior, wants to be treated like a slut. It just doesn't feel nice. And if the guy you're sleeping with is acting like you're something to use then lose, he'll most likely kick you to the curb faster than you can find your panties the moment he meets a woman he respects enough to call his girlfriend.

Be forewarned that while most guys have no qualms about jumping into bed with a woman they've just met, they often consider said woman to be a playmate, not a take-home-to-mom mate. One of our blog-submitters dated a guy who told her he'd dated more than one hundred fifty women, and then freaked out when she said she's slept with eight men, calling her a "sex fiend" and telling her he'd have to "discuss" her number with his female best friend. A guy once told Meagan she was lucky she didn't sleep with him right away because he wouldn't have dated her if she had. So, yes, it's a double standard, but men still judge us by it.

That said, some gals are fine with relationships based purely on sex—and more power to them. Go ahead, slut yourself silly. But this chapter is less about what you're doing and more about what he's doing. Regardless of when you sleep with your man or whether or not your relationship is "open," he should regard you as a valued individual, not a dishrag he can toss away. If your interactions with him make you feel shameful, it's likely because he's treating you like a slut.

A WORD ON
"The Love Hormone"

Some women are perfectly capable of casual sex, and therefore suffer no emotional fallout as long as the terms of the relationship are clear; and then there are those who think they are capable of having casual sex, only to find themselves doing whatever it takes to keep the guy around. The reason most women get so attached is partially scientific: While doing the deed, both men and women release oxytocin, a feel-good hormone that promotes social bonding. Dubbed "the love hormone," oxytocin's power increases tenfold in the presence of estrogen. So women bond faster and stronger than their male counterparts, creating a disparity in attachment levels between the sexes.

He cuts right to the chase.

Men have sex on their minds and sometimes they can't help but voice their carnal intentions. This is normal: A man's spoken desire to rip your clothes off may even turn you on. However, if all he seems to talk about from date one is getting you in his bed, he may take you for a floozy. When "let's get busy" comes before "what's your name?" it's a sign that he's only interested in getting to know you on a sexual, not personal, level.

> *Red-Flag Rule* #4: If he's hinting at not just a goodnight kiss, but a till-the-morning romp ten minutes into your first date, we guarantee he's looking for a bedmate, not a soul mate.

WTF? *"Recently, one of my girlfriends was on a dinner date with a man and upon finding out she wasn't going to have sex with him after— he left. Sticking her with the bill."*

First and foremost, to petition for sexual favors before getting to know a gal is not only inappropriate, but also totally disrespectful and misogynistic. It's hard to believe that men with this approach *ever* get laid. But, when they throw their noxious nets so far they're bound to get a few bites. These punks don't mind blatantly offending nine women, because the tenth might actually take the bait. A dude who's looking for a girlfriend wouldn't risk insulting you right off the bat. He'd work on getting to know you with your clothes *on* before trying to take them off.

BIG RED-FLAG STORY:

"You know it's a red-flag Internet dating moment when, on your first date all the guy talks about is the weird sex he had while in the Army. Then, when he finally drives you home (after singing a shitty, unsolicited rugby chant) he looks over at you and says, 'I'm hoping since we live near each other we can just get together for the sex. Are you okay with that?'"

His dick always comes first.

You could be having the worst day of your life—you just lost your job, your grandmother died, your car broke down, your own dog bit you in the ass—and he's still trying to make a move. Clearly, he doesn't care about you, and he doesn't even have the decency to give you time to recover before expecting you to attend to his sexual needs.

BIG RED-FLAG STORY:

"One of my friends was in a pretty bad car accident and ended up spending a weekend in the hospital. This guy she was hooking up with at the time went to visit her. Instead of just hanging out, keeping her company, or wishing her a speedy recovery, he tried to hump her! Absolutely inexcusable, especially considering her neck was in a traction device and both of her legs broken."

When his libido needs to be serviced before you can have a genuine conversation, you do not have a genuine dude: He's a big-headed, self-centered ass, and sees you as his servant, not his equal.

He thinks your body is always at his disposal.

There's something that just feels dirty about hooking up with a guy whose only interest in your body is using it to get himself off. You know the type: He treats your feminine parts like separate commodities put in place exclusively for his pleasure, with no regard for the woman they're attached to. He's not concerned with your satisfaction, only your willingness to let him satisfy himself.

Even if your relationship is largely sex-based, a man should still be interested in your comfort and pleasure. Without some tenderness, sex becomes more business transaction than intimate encounter . . . in which case, you may as well ask him to leave you a check by the nightstand.

WTF? *"Being in Spain, where they smoke in their sleep, I understood the need for this guy to finish his cigarette while I was giving him a blowjob. But I had to draw the line when he placed the ashtray on top of my head."*

BIG RED-FLAG STORY:

"Becoming intimate with this guy for the first time, I should have known his only concern was getting laid. After poking at my clit and prodding at my nipples for a total of ninety seconds, he apparently thought I was ready to be entered, and despite the discomfort that I'm sure was evident on my face, preceded to have sex with me for another ninety seconds. To finish he ripped off the condom, gave himself a hand job, and came on my breasts, which had been 'enhanced' years ago. As if I didn't feel disgusting enough, he asked, 'Is that what you got them for?' Yeah, I paid thousands of dollars and underwent major surgery just so some douchebag would have a place to ejaculate."

Being objectified is about as enjoyable as getting a double root canal. But while a root canal is sometimes necessary, staying with this dude is absolutely not. Find a man that wants *all* of you, not just your bodacious bod.

He's a late-night creeper.

You'd be surprised how many women confuse late-night hookups with actual relationships. You should know that if a guy's truly interested in you, he's going to take you out, not merely invite you to join him once he's already at the bar with his boys, or call you after midnight just to "see what you're up to." And if that's exactly what's going on, then you, my friend, are merely his last resort when he can't find another chick to take home.

Red-Flag Rule #5: If your "dates" with a guy consist solely of booze and booty calls, chances are he's not your boyfriend.

BIG RED-FLAG STORY:

"I asked the guy I was seeing what his plans were for the evening, and he said he was just going to 'lay low.' Imagine my surprise when, at nearly one in the morning, he showed up unannounced knocking on my front door, fresh from a night out with his men. While I was excited to see him at the time, I realize now I shouldn't have let him in."

The theory that if you hook up with a guy long enough he'll eventually become your boyfriend is hopeful but not sound. Though pillow talk is fun, it's usually not very concrete. There needs to be more to a relationship than what happens between midnight and the wee hours of the morning. Years ago, Julie spent several weeks hooking up with a guy before she realized that she didn't know anything about him, like where he grew up or how he pronounced his last name. Not surprisingly, without a firm base, the relationship never graduated from the dorm room to outside world.

He's not down for sleepovers.

You just had sex with a guy and, after laying naked together for a few minutes in post-orgasmic bliss, you head to the bathroom, do your thing, and when you come out . . . he's completely dressed. Before you can even register what's happening, he stutters some lame excuse and gives you a nod on his way out. Or perhaps you've had to scramble around naked looking for your clothes while the dude you just bedded stands impatiently by the front door. Either way, my dear, you have just been done and ditched.

While a guy may indeed have to "get up early" every once in a while, if he's not a sanitation worker, emergency room doctor, morning news anchor, or other off-hours wage earner, he has to get up the same time everyone else does. Regardless of the excuse for needing to sleep solo, if your man leaves, or expects you to leave, after a night of nookie, well, you can forget about becoming his girlfriend.

And if you insist on spending the night together against his wishes, you'll not only have an uncomfortable time sleeping next to a man who evidently wants nothing to do with you, but also a very awkward morning complete with a get-up-and-get-the-hell-out attitude from him.

> *Red-Flag Rule #6:* If he tells you he's got a "busy day"
> the moment his alarm goes off, don't expect him
> to take you to breakfast.

BIG RED-FLAG STORY:
This one comes straight from the source himself—and don't worry, he knows he committed quite the flag here.

"The next morning after a one-night stand, I was in bed—wide-awake—ready to start my day. (It was 10 A.M.) Soon enough, the chick I'd brought home the night before rolled over, looked at me and asked me what I was thinking. The conversation then went as follows:

Me: I'm ready to start my day, gotta get some stuff going.
Girl: Cool. [Rolls back over]
Me: Yeah, I gotta clean and do my laundry.
Girl: Great!
Me: I'm doing whites. [My sheets are white.]
Girl: Okay.
Me: Like now.

> Girl: Seriously? Can I get back into your freshly made
> bed after?
> Me: I'd rather you didn't.

"Listen, missy: You're not my girlfriend, nor an f-buddy, nor a good friend crashing in my bed, you are a one-night stand and no, you cannot get back in my freshly made bed. The reason I am washing my sheets is because of you. You don't know me, you should have snuck out hours ago—seriously, why are you still here? I made a mistake. I'm not buying you breakfast. Please leave."

THE BOTTOM LINE:

You're only a slut if the guy you're choosing to be sexually intimate with is treating you like one . . . and if you're letting him. It basically comes down to one thing: respect. If you feel like you're being respected, and have realistic expectations about where the relationship is headed, then, as a grown woman, you have the right to sleep with whomever you want and shouldn't be subjected to other people's judgment. But if you feel cheap, chances are the guy considers you just another slut for the taking.

Men will only respect you to the degree you respect yourself, so stand tall and have the self-confidence to demand the treatment you deserve.

TOP TEN RED FLAGS:
Where You Met Him

1. At work. He's your boss.
2. At a friend's bachelorette party. He stripped.

3. At your friend's birthday party. He was dating her . . . until he cheated with you later that night.
4. At home. He's your roommate.
5. At your door. He's a Jehovah's Witness.
6. At your family reunion. He may be a blood relative.
7. At the police station. He shared a cell with your ex.
8. At the local high school. He's your son's friend.
9. At a gay bar. But he's totally straight (you think).
10. At daycare. He was 500 feet outside the building due to a restraining order.

Chapter Three

He's a Player

From t-ball to table hockey to fantasy football, men love to play games. Hard-wired for competition, they can easily fall into the habit of treating a woman like just another notch in their headboards. Most often, it's not just about sex, but bragging rights, too.

But a guy who's slept with a lot of women isn't necessarily a player; if he's sleeping with several of them simultaneously, however, he is. When a man manipulates you into believing you're his one and only when you're actually his one of many, he's officially hit player status. Julie's college roommate was strung along for over a year by a guy who constantly swore that he was going to break up with his girlfriend to be with her, but never actually did, leaving her disappointed and drained.

> *Red-Flag Rule #7:* If a guy declares his love for you, and he's currently dating your best friend—run.

Falling victim is easier than it sounds because players are smooth— after all, they've been practicing since puberty. They know just what to say and do to make you think you've found your very own Prince

Charming—which is why it's hard to move on when you begin to recognize that your guy's more Don Juan than "happily ever after."

The truth is, if he sounds too good to be true, he probably is. This guy knows all the lines to lay on the charm and all the moves to make you swoon. It may sound like he's acting from the heart but, really, he's just acting.

So, keep a lookout for the signals below and have the self-confidence to move on and find a man who treats you like a precious gem, not just another rock to kick around.

He tracks his conquests.

If a guy is keeping a running list of the women he's "had," sex is obviously less about the individual girl and more about his ability to vanquish territory. We've heard of men keeping sex diaries detailing every intimate encounter they've had, and while a guy may track this info in his head, if he writes it down it may mean he anticipates his list will grow too long for him to remember. His behavior could also signal a deeper issue—seeing the number of women he's bedded in writing could help him reaffirm his masculinity and worth, characteristics that shouldn't revolve around sex.

BIG RED-FLAG STORY:

"I went to my guy's place for a date. He was in the shower so I used the key he gave me to let myself in—pretty routine. I hung out in his room (as usual) and went to the computer (as usual) to check my e-mail. When the screensaver lifted there was a document with a list of girls, all numbered. I was at the bottom, #16. Could have been a list of girlfriends, but sixteen seems like a lot for a guy who's only twenty-six, so was it a list of all the girls he'd slept with?"

He's shady with his phone (part I).

If he's always receiving calls in the middle of the night, and takes them in another room, or grabs his phone the second it rings in the hopes that you won't see the caller ID, he's probably not talking to his mother.

Don't fall for lines like "It's a work call" or "That's an old college friend," because he's probably telling the same exact thing to the other women he's seeing when you call. Often the amount of secret texts he sends is directly related to how many women he's sleeping with. (For more on this topic, see Chapter 15.)

BIG RED-FLAG STORY:

"I went on a date with a guy and he spent literally half the time texting. We'd be in the middle of a conversation and he'd just start typing. I asked if something was wrong because he was glancing at the phone every few seconds and typing intensely, but he said 'no,' he 'just liked to be informed.' So then I informed him that he was being insanely rude. He got pissed and revealed that he had been texting a 'backup' because I seemed 'too girl next door' to have sex with him on a first date and he really needed to get laid."

Don't be the paranoid broad who checks her man's voicemail or text messages: It only makes you look crazy, deflecting the blame from his shadiness to your distrustful nature. The only thing you can do is ask him if he's chatting up other chicks. From there, your options are to believe him or leave him. End of story.

He's inflexible with his time.

If planning a date with your dude is more complicated than nuclear physics and he gives you weekly time slots that he can "fit you into," he's probably fitting himself into a myriad of women (if you know what we mean). If he's inflexible with his time, don't be so flexible with your legs.

BIG RED-FLAG STORY:
"I was out at a bar and saw a guy I recently went out on a date with. He mentioned maybe getting together the following afternoon since he would be in my neighborhood. I didn't hear from him all of the next day. Then, he called at five P.M. asking me to meet him sometime between five-thirty and eight P.M. I told him I'd already made plans for the night so we'd have to meet up another time. He proceeded to give me shit about how he was offering me a two-hour window and that I needed to work around that."

Since a player is experienced in the art of deception, he'll convince you that his time is limited because he's such a good person— hard-working, family-oriented, and loyal. Likewise, common excuses will be late meetings with a coworker, his younger brother's soccer games, or dinners with a friend in crisis. When you ask to meet said coworker, brother, or best friend, you may be able to catch a wrinkle of worry on his face, but it will quickly fade as he coolly replies that his coworker is so boring you'd never want to hang with him, his brother has Asperger's, and his friend just left the country for a few months. Don't buy his bull.

A man who wants you in his life will not just fit you in, but plan around you, no matter how busy he is. Even if he's not spending his time with other women, what's the point of seeing someone if you never get to actually see them? Sure, if you're in a long-term com- mitted relationship you may make an exception, but this shouldn't be his M.O. from the start.

He's too good to be true.

Unlike the cut-to-the-chase fella in the previous chapter, a player won't lay his carnal intentions out on the table during the first date. Instead, he'll tell you everything he thinks you, and all women, want to hear. A too-good-to-be-true player will set you up to fall hard with lines like "I've never felt this way before," knowing the harder you fall the less likely you are to get up and walk away. Every time you grow suspicious, he hopes you'll think back on the romantic things he's said or done and decide that your gut has just got to be off.

We've got news for you: A woman's intuition is her best defense against getting played. Don't deny common sense—you'll just end up kicking yourself down the road when your gut feeling is confirmed.

BIG RED-FLAG STORY:

"I was dating this guy I really liked. He said he was incredibly into me too and wanted to wait until we knew each other better before we had sex. I took that as a sign of a gentleman. I enjoyed his company and was kinda falling for him, especially when he indicated that he wanted me to move in after just six weeks of dating. Then, one night he picked me up for a date and said he had a gift for me. I opened the little box to find a gold pig charm on a chain—it was an odd choice but a cute little necklace. It was a sweet gesture and I loved it.

"About a month later my roommate came home flustered after a dinner with some of her girlfriends. Her friend was going on and on about this handsome new boyfriend that she had been dating for a couple of months. Not only was he good looking and intelligent, he had just given her the cutest pig necklace.

"Now normally my roommate would not have said anything, but the pig necklace was far too coincidental. So she asked the chick to see a photo of the guy and, yup—you got it—it was the guy I was dating. I phoned him the next day to find out just how many more little piggies he had floating around."

When it feels like your relationship with a guy is in fast-forward, hit pause and re-evaluate the reasons he claims to be so into you. If he never offers concrete reasons why you're specifically the one, he's trying to manipulate you into dropping your drawers. Since players are adept at reading and maneuvering women's emotions, keep yourself in check: Focus on what you like about him besides his promises of 2.5 beautiful children he'll send to the best private schools.

He's not interested in getting to know you.

While players will talk about the far-off future you supposedly have together, they usually avoid discovering you in the present. If your guy's not asking the basic questions, like how many siblings you have or what hobbies you enjoy, it may be because he's only interested knowing you in the biblical sense. When you voluntarily offer info, he'll likely feign concern but then quickly move to the physical. For example, you tell him you had a bad day and he'll say, "I'm sorry babe," move in for a kiss, and whisper, "Why don't you let me make it all better?" And within minutes you're getting busy.

BIG RED-FLAG STORY:

"I started chatting with a guy through an online dating service. He said he used to work in the fashion industry but recently quit. When I asked why, he told me he'd rather we were closer to one another before he shared this personal detail.

"Despite being sketchy about the job thing, we sort of hit it off and decided to talk on the phone. He called that night, less than twenty-four hours after we'd first made contact online. He told me how much he wanted to kiss me and asked if I wanted to hear the fantasy he had about me earlier in the day. I found this an odd topic for a first conversation but was even more shocked when he told me he was going to take his profile off the dating site for me because he thought we had a real shot at a future together.

"Later on in the same call, he tried to get me to have phone sex. A little job info was too personal, but phone sex was fine?"

A WORD ON
Serial Daters

Sometimes a guy doesn't display the typical player behavior we've already covered, but goes through girlfriends faster than you go through tampons on a heavy day. He'll get to know you and he won't mess around with other gals, but after a few times in the sack, he'll sack you and immediately move into another relationship. You may notice that his friends make no effort to get to know you: This is because they know he'll have a new girlfriend next week. If his list of exes is longer than the side effects in a drug commercial, he's probably looking to lay you then leave you.

He tells you he's a player.

Red-Flag Rule #8: If he explicitly says, "I'm never going to be the boyfriend type," take his word for it and find a more loyal lad.

While this one seems obvious, we've talked to a lot of women who've ignored this flag because they thought they could "fix" a guy's wanton ways. The he'll-change-for-me attitude is certainly romantic, but the odds are not in your favor. Whether he tells you he's a player directly or hints at it, he's doing it so that he can say he warned you when you find out he's hooking up with multiple chicks or when he refuses to let you call him your boyfriend.

Perhaps a player's appeal is not that you want to fix him, but that he presents a challenge. If it's less about the actual guy and more about competing with other women, join a softball team—winning a plastic trophy will be far more rewarding than winning a guy you don't really like in the first place.

BIG RED-FLAG STORY:

"You know a guy's interested in you when there's heavy flirting, lingering eye contact, playful touching of the legs, back, and waist, and so forth. Well, I was pretty sure this guy and I were possibly going to start something up. That was until he felt the need to tell me that he met a ton of women daily at the gym he owned and that his friends were trying to set him up with a whole bunch more. Clearly this guy's ego was in need of some serious stroking. If he flirts heavily enough to indicate he's interested in you, but doesn't show any interest in dating you, he's doing the same with every girl he meets—and apparently he meets a lot of women."

THE BOTTOM LINE:

While immature men may think that being a player is cool, it's really a form of misogyny: Players work to establish control over a woman's emotions in order to manipulate or use her. Even if a guy's debonair attitude seems to speak otherwise, you'll most likely never be more than an object to him and your feelings won't factor into the relationship, leaving you hurt and violated.

Players prey on the most susceptible women—they sense low self-esteem and know how to make you feel like you're wanted and loved.

When you realize that's not the case, your self-esteem drops even lower, creating a dangerous cycle. If you keep ending up in this situation, it may be time to take a break from dating and work on your confidence so that you can separate bullshit sweet talk from genuine conversation and learn to trust your intuition. After all, the best way to avoid being hurt by players is not to fall for them in the first place.

An honest man will ask questions about your goals, dreams, and desires but he typically won't promise to fulfill them before getting to know you on a deeper level. A guy who focuses on the future, instead of learning about you in the present, is looking to charm you into the bedroom, not into his life. Remember, there will always be players, but you can opt not to play their games.

TOP TEN RED FLAGS:
His Reason for Dating You

1. He's trying to "hit" every ethnicity.
2. He wants to beat his buddy's "number."
3. He has nothing better to do.
4. Your biorhythms align well.
5. He's moving next week and needs help.
6. You remind him of his sister.
7. He's "got a thing for big girls."
8. Your brother has weed.
9. Jesus told him to.
10. He has an albino fetish. (You, however, are not albino, just pale.)

He May Like Men

You may be thinking: Wouldn't I know if I was dating a gay guy? Sure, sometimes you can tell a man is into dudes within a few minutes of talking to him. But sexuality isn't always an open-and-shut case and, therefore, neither is determining a man's sexual orientation.

We know men who religiously tune in to *Gossip Girl,* own more pink clothing than a newborn baby girl, and spend hours getting ready every morning who are, in fact, not gay. Conversely, we also know meat-and-potato, football-on-Sundays, what-are-you-wearing-are-you-colorblind manly guys who are 100 percent into dudes. Then there are the fellas who're still figuring it out, those whose preference seems to change with the flavor of the week, and those who just aren't interested in intimacy, period. So, no, you may not know if your guy prefers muscled chests to your breasts.

This chapter is not intended to fuel stereotypes, but rather to help you recognize when the guy you're lusting after may be lusting after someone else . . . someone male. And while we love gay men, we don't recommend choosing one as your boyfriend.

Dating a guy who doesn't seem to be truly into you or your body can wreak havoc on your self-esteem. We know a woman who slept in the buff next to her boyfriend almost every night for an entire year without having sex. Ever. Sure, he would hold her and rub her back, doing those kinds of comforting things we all wish our boyfriends would do, but they never actually "did it." Here she'd found a seemingly perfect boyfriend in every way and while their relationship started off hot and heavy, things quickly dissipated in the bedroom.

At first, she thought he might be experiencing a problem with his man tool, but he never actually divulged why he wasn't interested in having sex. She came to the logical assumption that her vagina must have been no good and spent several months in therapy and at the gynecologist, her sexual self-esteem crushed. While they're no longer together, and she still doesn't know for sure if he's gay, his lack of intimacy certainly created a very unhealthy relationship.

Whether interested in other men, other women, or squirrels, if a guy's heart, head, or hard-on is elsewhere, he's not 100 percent committed to you, nor being 100 percent honest with you. Since commitment and honesty are the glue of any strong relationship, yours will eventually fracture without them.

Everyone thinks he's gay.

If your man registers on literally every person's gaydar but your own, it's likely that yours is broken. While the snap judgments of acquaintances can certainly be ignored, if people who know him well, like his friends and family (or even your own), all seem to concur that he's a same-sex subscriber, you may simply be blinded by love.

BIG RED-FLAG STORY:

"Everyone thought my friend's father, who was married with three children, was gay. While some of this speculation was based on stereotypes—he knitted, sang show tunes, and baked—some came from other parents who knew him on a more personal level. While we were in high school, he had an affair . . . with a man. Shortly thereafter her parents got divorced and he officially came out. I can't say that anyone was very shocked."

Gay men who aren't out often feel pressured to pursue relationships with women. Some may even be brainwashed into thinking they can change their preference simply by dating girls. And a lot of women will stick with a guy they think may be gay similarly believing they'll be the woman to set him straight—literally. As hard as a dude like this tries to like chicks, and as hard as you try to make him like chicks, science simply doesn't work in your favor.

He tells you he's bi.

We don't deny that some men do indeed lust after Will *and* Grace, but research done in 2010 by the gay-and-bi-friendly dating site OKCupid.com suggests a disparity between those who self-identify as bi and those who are not out yet.

After studying one and a half million users, the site found that 80 percent of people who labeled themselves "bi" were almost exclusively reading the profiles of, and sending messages to, one gender. OKCupid also looked at users over time and noticed that many of the men who had identified as bisexual in their teens and twenties changed their profiles to say "gay" by their mid-thirties, leading the study to conclude that the bi label may simply be a caution taken by those that are not yet out.

So we're not saying a man can't be bi, or that a man is definitely gay if he says he bats for both teams, we're just letting you know that if he identifies himself as bisexual and you'd prefer that he's just into girls, well, he's not.

BIG RED-FLAG STORY:

"I went on a date with a guy I met online. Based on his profile, he seemed cool. Ten minutes after we met, he told me that there was something I should know. Turned out he was bisexual. Okay, I could keep an open mind. Then, right after we ordered drinks, he let it slip that he was currently in a relationship with a man. Now, that was the sort of thing I'd like to have known before meeting (I am not interested in becoming somebody's secondary partner or beard). Shortly thereafter, my date received a phone call from the aforementioned boyfriend, who proceeded to dump him, right then and there, for being out on a date with a woman."

He's obsessed with a male friend.

It's totally normal for a guy to admire a male friend or even have a bit of bromance brewing. While brewing is fine, marinating in man love is not. Your guy's habit of bragging about his bro could turn annoying and even distressing. If he blathers on and on like a tween reading *Tiger Beat* and ditches date night to hang with his homie, your guy may not just admire his friend, but actually have the hots for him. Perhaps he doesn't realize this and won't even act on it, but the time, energy, and googly-eyed sighs he's spending on his man crush should be focused on you.

BIG RED-FLAG STORY:

"My boyfriend became obsessed with this famous dude he became acquainted with and tried to convince everybody they were best friends. (Red flag in itself.) I knew something was very wrong when he told me that being away from the guy was like 'coming down from a high' (um, he never did a drug in his life) and how he was 'miserable' without him. We were trying to maintain a long-distance relationship (across the country) at the time and he didn't seem to be experiencing withdrawal from me. His girlfriend."

He's obsessed with specific body parts.

We'll be very direct: We're talking bums and peckers. If a guy is really into your butt or his butt—and we mean *really* into either (e.g., he asks you to spread your cheeks so he can stare at your anus for ten minutes—real story) or he's ultra curious about other dudes' penises (e.g., he asks your friends the length and girth of their boyfriend's rods—also a real story), this may be a sign that he's interested in exploring territories beyond your vagina (and perhaps beyond your body altogether). While anal play doesn't equal gay, if he can't get hard without having you finger his butt when you get busy, that may be a problem. (For more, check out Chapter 10).

A WORD ON
Gay Bashing

While blatant homophobia doesn't necessarily mean a man is secretly gay, there is an obvious correlation between the two—just look at the number of anti-gay male politicians who turn out to actually like men themselves. In an effort to hide their sexuality and appear as straight as possible, closeted men often overcompensate. They don't just dislike gay culture—they despise it. Gay couples don't make them uncomfortable, they make them physically ill. Gay marriage doesn't just irk them, it sends them on all-out rants. If this sounds like your guy, you may just be dating an asshole, or you could be dating a closeted gay.

BIG RED-FLAG STORY:

"The last year I was with my ex-boyfriend (we were together five years) he would only have sex with me if we did it doggie style. At the time, I kept my hair in the back shaved down, and during sex he would constantly say, 'The back of your head is so hot!' I ignored it until he told me that he wished he were gay."

He plays with gays.

A lot of straight men have gay friends: It's no big deal. Having pals of all types shows your man is both tolerant and accepting. Plus, since gay men tend to have lots of female friends, your guy's pal may be able to help him better understand where you're coming from and what you want out of the relationship (including, but not limited to, massages, jewelry, and orgasms).

But if every one of a dude's friends seems to go for guys, you may have a closet case on your hands. It's cool if he wants to attend an LGBT pride parade but another thing if he wants to dress like a drag queen and dance to ABBA on a float with his gay friends.

Red-Flag Rule #9: If he's overly eager to engage in gay culture, he may also be overly eager to engage in gay coitus.

While sexual exploration is healthy, he shouldn't be lollygagging with gay men when he's dating you. If a typical Saturday night features you playing Photo Hunt in the corner of a gay bar while your man flits about like he's just found the land of milk and honey, we're sorry to say that he may be stringing you along until he can solidify his sexuality. Even if it's unintentional, his behavior is unfair and hurtful. When his gay clique becomes more interesting to him than your clit, for your own sake, you need to go find a man who is sure of his straightness.

BIG RED-FLAG STORY:

"I planned to hang out with my friends and go to one of the local gay bars, and I decided to bring along the guy I was currently seeing. The night was going well until we were outside smoking, and he whispered, 'I have bisexual tendencies.' I honestly didn't know how to react. Then, after leaving the club, a bunch of us went to a friend's house to have an after-hours thing. All the guys (who were all gay, I should add) decided to strip to their underwear and go swimming. I didn't go in because I wasn't feeling well, but without a second of hesitation, my guy stripped down and jumped in with them. All night he pretty much ignored me and hung out with the guys, and, come to find out the next morning, he actually went skinny dipping with them."

THE BOTTOM LINE:

Women often have a strong hunch that they're dating a gay man, but have trouble admitting it to themselves, probably because gay men and straight women get along so darn well. Dating a gay man may be temporarily fulfilling, but he'll never be able to meet all of your emotional and physical needs. If you get the feeling he's more into the *idea* of you than the actual you, it could kick the crap out of your confidence, setting you up for failure in future relationships.

TOP TEN RED FLAGS:
His Pet Name For You

1. Jim
2. Pudge
3. Hey, you
4. Saggytits
5. Plan B
6. Wifey
7. Stinky
8. Snaggletooth
9. Dude
10. Babushka

WHILE THE LAST CHAPTER may seem different than the others in this part, it's the same at the core: Whether a man won't DTR, treats you like a slut, acts like a player, or is a closeted gay, he can't offer you the traditional things we expect when we partner up: honesty, concern, and support. There's nothing more frustrating than giving 100 percent and getting 50 in return.

Stop hoping he'll change: Daydreaming about your calculating or confused guy down on one knee is the work of Hollywood, which grossly overestimates how many men actually recognize they're being jerks, let alone transform themselves for a woman. Your best bet is to cut your losses and find someone who can honestly commit to not just knocking boots, but also being called your boyfriend.

Red-Flag Case Study #1

See how many red flags you can spot in just one story:

"Having always been fairly introverted, during my first semester in college I made a serious attempt to come out of my shell. I became friends with some guys who I thought were really cool, and developed a major crush on one of them. The boy was cute, smart, and musically gifted. Dream guy, right? We started hanging out and sometimes he would kiss me, but only after smoking pot. The next day he would make it a point to say that the only reason we'd kissed was because he'd been smoking, in case I didn't already realize this.🚩 Like an idiot, I thought that maybe if I gave him time he would revert back to the guy I thought he was when I started crushing on him.🚩

"Wrong. A few weeks later I ended up staying at his place. We were watching a movie and started making out.🚩 After I refused to let him go further, he went to jerk off in the bathroom while I cried on his couch.🚩 I found out later that he told our mutual friends that we'd slept together.🚩 Needless to say, I've kept my distance since then."

🚩 He has to be high to make out. That's a pretty big problem.

🚩 He's not really into her and he's letting her know. If a guy tells you he doesn't like you—believe him!

🚩 He's not going to change. Her hopeful inner voice is saying that he might but she shouldn't listen to it.

🚩 He's a user. She should have realized what she was getting herself into, but he should've been man enough not to take advantage of her.

🚩 He's selfish and has absolutely no concern for her emotions.

🚩 He's a liar.

Part Two
He Needs to Grow Up

Chapter Five

He Acts
Like a Child

Dating a man who behaves like a kid can make you feel like you actually have a kid. Except this one is bigger and hairier, and you can't put him in cute little outfits.

We're not talking about a guy's childlike hobbies, such as building rockets well into his thirties or collecting comic books well into his forties—if we were going to count those sorts of things as red flags we'd be hard-pressed to find any marriageable men at all.

We're more concerned about the juvenile tendencies woven into a guy's general conduct that can affect—and often disrupt—the very fabric of your relationship. While you may be slightly disturbed watching your man curse into his video game headset (especially when many of his Halo opponents are in middle school), as long as his pastimes don't change his everyday demeanor and treatment of you, your man can nerd it up all he wants.

That said, you can't have an equal partnership with a guy who acts more like your little brother than your boyfriend. Here are some signs that your guy needs to pull up his big-boy panties or suffer an infinite time-out.

He's embarrassing.

Just as kids don't typically know how to properly behave, some grown men don't either—usually because no one has ever taught them or they've chosen not to learn. Or they just don't give a fuck.

Misguided, and typically not discreet, a childlike guy can embarrass you a number of ways, like loudly recounting offensive jokes or engaging in potty humor during a candlelit dinner in a fancy restaurant. Or he may act in ways that most adults just wouldn't while in public. Running around Victoria's Secret with a bra on his head would be cute if he was two, and maybe funny if he was twelve, but is completely horrifying if he's thirty. This "boy" has no boundaries, and he's not likely to respect those of others, yours included. Like a live grenade carried in your purse, this dude will always have you on edge, waiting for him to go off at an inopportune time, like during your boss's promotion party or your godson's christening.

As Natasha well knows, there's nothing worse than introducing your boyfriend to your friends or family, only to be thoroughly humiliated by him. Her ex-boyfriend had a nose-picking habit so bad that her parents had to sit her down for a serious talk about why she was dating him. How, they wondered, could she even consider spending her life with a guy whose digits were permanently jammed up his beak?

When she told her nostril-excavating beau that she'd like him to get rid of this unsanitary habit, he retorted that he could pick his nose in public if he felt like it. And while that was certainly true, she wasn't sure why a guy would feel the need to be so defensive of his right to dig for boogers. Nose picking in itself may seem like a superficial red flag, albeit a gross one, but the behavior (and the protection thereof) indicated the guy was immature, stubborn, and disrespectful. Qualities we'd all prefer to do without.

Any guy who gives himself permission to do something obnoxious or offensive because he "feels like it" will be impossible to deal with on a daily basis. When everything your man does is justified with some self-serving pretext, he'll quickly wear down your patience until it's tissue-paper thin.

BIG RED-FLAG STORY:
"My ex-boyfriend used to slap my ass in public—hard—despite my clear and consistent demands that he refrain from doing so. In fact, when I'd tell him to stop, he'd get mad at me and say that I was 'too uptight.' Right, because most women want to be spanked while waiting in line at Starbucks."

WTF? *One afternoon, the guy I was dating and I went to lunch with my roommate, who is a cute girl with huge boobs. During the meal, she got crumbs all over the front of her shirt, mostly in her awesome-boob region. Because she and I are super close, I pointed to the crumbs and brushed them off of her shirt/boobs with my hand. Then, the guy I was dating decided to reach over me to 'wipe off some more crumbs'—i.e., grope her breasts—even though there were no crumbs left, giving both of us this sheepish 'What?' smile when he was finished.*

He's irresponsible.

We're not talking about forgetting to pay child support or the electric bill here (though, don't you worry, we will later), but the kind of behavior that tells you a man is just plain lazy—and juvenile—when it comes to his outlook on life. For example, we know a guy who refused to apply to more than one law school because he didn't want to "fill out all those long applications." Give us a break, dude.

One of the most attractive qualities a man can possess is drive. Laziness, therefore, is next to undateable-ness. If your man's idea of "getting his life together" is spending fourteen hours of every day at the gym, he's not exactly what we'd consider marriage, or even boyfriend, material. It's really unsexy (and annoying) when a guy acts like the laws of time don't apply to him and that despite everyone else thinking about their future, he can ignore it because he'll live happily ever after as a lost boy in Neverland. No career, no direction, no prospects . . . no thank you.

Some men are actually motivated but they lack realistic or practical goals. When Julie was in college, keeping with her tradition of dating non-Jews (despite her mom's pleas), she brought home a dreamy surfer dude with blue eyes, golden locks, and a tiny goy nose. Since a Jewish mother can't wait five minutes without finding out if her daughter's potential suitor is pursuing a respectable field (i.e., law, medicine, or finance), her mom asked him what he was majoring in. He responded, "Pre-med." But just as her parents breathed an audible sigh of relief, he followed up with "But that's not what I really want to do. I just want to surf."

While passion is sexy, there's a big difference between a guy who skateboards in his spare time, or joins a heavy metal band as a hobby, and a man who refuses to work so he can dedicate his entire life to pursuing his dreams of becoming Tony Hawk or Bon Jovi. While we're all for being supportive, your guy's plans for the future must have some roots in reality if you plan to grow together.

A mirage-chasing man offers no support when adult problems arise because he's never actually held a real job, paid taxes, bought a car, etc., and can't contribute sound advice on any of these topics (more on this in Chapter 8). Tell him you need his input on how to ask for a raise, and he'll likely respond with "Wear something slutty." Thanks, buddy—huge help. A thirteen-year-old could have offered a more complex suggestion.

BIG RED-FLAG STORY:
"I met this guy who is convinced that he's going to be a video game designer. His qualifications for this position? He likes to play video games. Yeah. He never went to college, doesn't know how to design anything, can't hold a job, lives with his friend's parents, and doesn't own a cell phone."

He acts like girls have cooties.

Red-Flag Rule #10: If a guy can't hear the word "vagina" without giggling, he should not be permitted to touch yours.

If our blog readers' story submissions are any indication, there are a lot of guys out there who just can't deal with female body functions. We're talking about men (boys) who freak out if they see a woman breastfeeding and have to change the channel when a Vagisil commercial comes on TV.

These alleged "men" cringe the most when we mention anything about our regular visits from Aunt Flo. (How conveniently guys seem to forget that we bleed from the vagina every month.) We're not saying that a guy can't complain if you forget to wrap up your maxi pad before putting it in his bathroom trash can, but your man should be able to pick you up a box of tampons from the drugstore without needing a cootie shot.

BIG RED-FLAG STORY:

"I was over at my boyfriend's house when I unexpectedly got my period . . . all over his sheets. I was obviously mortified. I know guys freak out when they even hear about menstruation so I didn't expect him to be calm, cool, and collected, but I also didn't expect him to call me 'absolutely disgusting' and demand that I pay him for the sheets (which I would have done anyway) on the spot."

He's still exploring his body.

When young boys discover their bodies, they play with certain parts no matter if they're in the privacy of their Batman-wallpapered bedrooms or in the grocery store with their moms. A natural part of male development is figuring out what's up with that strange little stub bellow their belly button.

Some guys, however, never grow out of touching their frank and/or beans every chance they get. We know a girl who dated a chronic ball-tugger. They would be sitting in the living room for a night of Tivo and take-out when she'd find him with his hand down his pants. This wasn't routine adjusting, and he wasn't arousing himself, he just liked to tug at the skin covering his testicles because it "felt good." While this tendency isn't destructive, if your guy is twenty-five and still exploring his body like a curious toddler, something's a little off.

And while we're at it, picking at scabs, calling attention to the oozing fungus between his toes, or showing you how much earwax he got on a Q-tip are similarly immature actions. We've seen it before and don't need to see it again. Thank you very much, sir. Any dude who still laughs when he farts, or even runs over to pass gas on your lap, has the comedic taste of a preschooler. Good luck having a conversation with a guy who interrupts you midsentence to belch and blow it in your face.

BIG RED-FLAG STORY:

"Before jumping into the shower one morning my now ex-boyfriend said he wanted to show me something. He came over to me, whipped out his penis, and pulled his foreskin back in order to show me his smegma-ring. Obviously his doing so was unsolicited—and his smegma was definitely something I did not want to have to see, ever."

He's emotionally infantile.

We love men who emote, who are sensitive, who make us feel less crazy for feeling so much. While it's certainly not a red flag for a man to cry from time to time, there's a line: If he sobs on your shoulder every night about completely nonsensical things, like his sister being taller than him, his friend beating him during the finals of a beer pong tournament, or his inability to make a fading jump shot (all true stories), he's crossed it. A real man won't scream things like "DON'T MESS WITH ME IN THIS GAME OR IN LIFE" at his sister-in-law while playing *Monopoly* (also a true story). Or tease you about your muffin top. Or whine when he's hungry. And so on.

Furthermore, if he blubbers when his favorite pair of jeans shrink, how do you think he'll handle real problems like unplanned pregnancy or unanticipated debt? You need a man to lean on in turbulent times, not one who'll topple over the second you rest your arm on his shoulder.

BIG RED-FLAG STORY:

"My boyfriend wanted to go to Orlando for his twenty-first birthday and the plan was to spend the weekend visiting Universal Studios and Disney World. At one of the parks, he won a huge bikini-clad stuffed penguin. When I suggested giving it to a little kid, he refused and proceeded to carry it around with us all day. In fact, when he flew back home at the end of the trip, the penguin, which he named Oscar Wally, got his own seat in business class."

He's a stage-five clinger.

Relationships work best when two people have their own, independent lives apart from the one they share. A man shouldn't need you to continually entertain him or spend every second with him. You signed up to be your guy's girlfriend, partner, or wife, not his security blanket. Think about whether his attachment is because he loves spending time with you or because he needs you to navigate each day. If it's the latter, you're more compass than companion.

BIG RED-FLAG STORY:

"I'd been dating a guy for five months when he began to get a little clingy. At first it was cute: He'd surprise me with lunch at work a few days a week or suggest running our weekend errands together. But soon, it got annoying. Why did he need to sit in the nail salon while I got a pedicure? And why couldn't I do my own food shopping? And why did I have to attend every single boring business school event he had?"

A boyfriend who insists on joining you absolutely everywhere—from your gyno visit to your all-female book club—is suffocating. Absence makes the heart grow fonder, but being attached at the hip makes the heart grow apathetic. Since carrying a giant man beast along with you all day is tiresome, we suggest you drop the dead weight off at his mommy's house so she can reattach him to her uterine wall.

THE BOTTOM LINE:

The immature behavior a childish man displays will no doubt affect your relationship with him. His adolescent tendencies will work their way into your day-to-day—namely in how your guy reacts to life's many surprises, how he deals with conflict, and how he conducts himself around you and others.

WTF? *"Years ago I met a great guy. We never connected because we were both taken, then we moved across the country from each other and lost touch. Years later, through the miracles of Facebook, I was able to reconnect with the 'one that got away.' He came down for a long weekend and things were going great: amazing sex, great food, plans for the future, and lots of laughs. We were having so much fun that we decided to hit up an old haunt for drinks. That's when things changed. He got completely trashed in an hour, picked fights with random strangers, and after staggering to my house, passed out cold. Sitting in the living room, I heard a strange sound, like a water fountain. I went into my room and realized that he had pissed all over my room in his sleep. I was cleaning up after him until four in the morning. Things were pretty awkward the next day before he left."*

A dude who refuses to adjust to the norms and values of society doesn't see youth as a stage, but rather a refuge from responsibility. The relationship isn't about you and him, it's about you acquiescing to him. An infantile man will take everything you offer and only ask for more, as if he's entitled to your daily devotion. The danger here is that you may have to hold up not just your end of the relationship bargain, but his as well. This will only reinforce his childish behavior, ensuring that he never learns to be a real contributor to your partnership. It's hard enough to make a romance work with two adults. Upping the challenge by dating an emotional ant is not recommended.

TOP TEN RED FLAGS:
His Habit of Choice

1. Picking his zits
2. Farting in enclosed spaces
3. Talking in the third person
4. Sleeping with exes
5. Scratching his foot with his fork
6. Using text speak in verbal conversations ("OMG I totally LMAO!")
7. Shaving his entire body (not related to playing sports)
8. Correcting your grammar
9. Talking over you when you're telling a story
10. Addictions: gambling, drugs, sex, alcohol, tanning, texting, table tennis, trigonometry, tangerines, Tolstoy (Obviously, any addiction is a red flag.)

Chapter Six

He's a
Momma's Boy

Behind every good man, you'll most likely find a mother who raised her child to respect and cherish women. Behind every momma's boy, however, you'll most likely find an overbearing woman who thinks you'll never be good enough for her son.

Despite their ability to grow facial hair, a momma's boy is just that—a boy—whose identity is still attached by the umbilical cord to his mother. While there's something endearing about a man who adores his mom, there's something slightly emasculating about a man who still consults mommy on his choice of underwear.

A momma's boy will forever be at his mother's beck and call, regardless of how intimate you become with her son. One of our reader's boyfriends would even pick up his mom's calls when they were in bed, about to get busy. This young woman knew she had made the right decision to let him go when, as they were breaking up, he paused the conversation to text—you guessed it—his mother.

The thing that sucks most about being in a relationship with a momma's boy is having to constantly compete for your man's attention—even if the "other woman" is his mom. A man may be beholden to the opinions of, and seek approval from, anyone in his family, but we've found that most momma's boys attach themselves to the woman whose breasts they once suckled.

He tells his mom everything.

Momma's boys are in constant communication with their mothers. You may not realize it, but if you're dating one, his mom probably knows every intimate detail of your relationship, and takes liberty to weigh in on every argument the two of you have. Chances are, you'll have to listen to her opinion—a momma's boy isn't shy about voicing what's on his mommy's mind.

Finding out your boyfriend has been discussing intimate details of you relationship—or even your sex life—with his mom feels like outright betrayal. But he may see the situation differently. He likely assumes that every guy tells his mom about his girlfriend's lingerie preferences. Assure him that this is not the case and make it crystal clear that certain bits of information, namely anything remotely sexual in nature or related to your heated disagreements, should always be kept on the DL. If he gets defensive or the habit proves too engrained to break, seriously consider whether you can deal with a threesome or want a partnership.

The "don't tell mommy dearest everything" rule applies to both parties: If you want him to be mum to mom, you must do so as well. At some point we all need to have separate lives from our parents, which is impossible when mom's the one you or your man speed-dial the moment you get a raise, a parking ticket, or a stomach bug.

BIG RED-FLAG STORY:
"My guy is a total momma's boy. He cries for no reason and defers to his mom about almost everything. Whenever we're fighting, he'll take up any chance to bring his mom into it. His mom, to

make matters worse, is a scheming and manipulative woman. She'll say something to your face and something else behind your back. And she's completely overbearing: at an exhibition hosted at my college, in front of my teacher and our families and friends, she actually spoon-fed my boyfriend, cooing to him like he was a baby."

He can't make a decision without her.

You may have thought it was cute when your now-boyfriend asked his mom where he should take you on your first date, but when you come to realize that he calls her several times a day to run every little decision by her, you might begin to wonder if his balls have dropped. Grown men respect their mothers' opinions; momma's boys can't make a move without their mothers' approval. Even when a mother-dependent guy knows his mom won't necessarily condone his actions, he'll check in with her anyway, seeking validation (or maybe he just fancies a spanking).

While a pushy or overbearing man is a turn-off, a decisive man is a total turn-on. We like a confident guy who can stand on his own two feet, not one who needs mommy as a crutch. If he doesn't trust himself to make his own choices, how does he expect you to trust him? As his girlfriend, you should be the one your lily-livered boy comes to for help making important decisions. And when his decisions are inconsequential, like whether he should buy Froot Loops or Lucky Charms, he should have the balls to make choices on his own.

BIG RED-FLAG STORY:
"For our one-year anniversary my boyfriend and I decided to go out for a nice dinner then get a hotel room. We were virgins

at the time and very excited to take the big step. For the entire week before the actual date, we were both extremely pumped and he kept repeating how much he couldn't wait to be with me. Halfway through our romantic dinner he informed me that the hotel plan was off because his mom didn't like the idea of him spending the night with a girl. Why he even mentioned the plan to her is a mystery to me. I'd thought the relationship was between him and myself, not him, myself, and his mom."

He shrinks under her command.

A mother knows she's done a good job when her son is able to flee the nest and navigate his own life. But momma's boys, if able to leave the nest at all, will always act as though they're under their mom's jurisdiction, obeying her every word. If he can't stand up to momma bear, he's not going to stand up for you when the time comes. Whether his family doesn't approve of your relationship or his mother simply doesn't like you, a momma's boy won't question the ruling, leaving you to feel insignificant in comparison.

> *Red-Flag Rule #11:* A guy who's not man enough to have your back on all occasions, even if it means upsetting his mother, isn't worth keeping around.

Based on pretty much every Disney movie ever produced, women want a strong, virile, knight-in-shining-armor, dragon-slaying, ax-wielding man, not a castrated pansy who bows down to his mother like she's a queen. And guess what? A man who's too chickenshit to stand up to his five-foot, hundred-pound mother doesn't have the intestinal fortitude to get ahead in the real world.

BIG RED-FLAG STORY:

"At twenty-nine (and living with his mom) my ex-boyfriend still had a curfew and wasn't allowed to have company over without his mother's permission, so we would often get a cheap hotel room to do our thing. One of those nights he locked the keys in his mother's car (because he didn't have one of his own), and proceeded to panic. Once I told him everything would be fine, we called a tow truck and decided to go have sex while we waited. Soon after, the doors were opened, keys recovered, and we were on our way back to his place.

"As soon as we walked into the apartment his mom popped off the couch and promptly told me I had to leave because she didn't allow 'females' in her apartment. So I politely asked her, 'How am I supposed to get home since your son picked me up from work?' She told me it wasn't her problem, and my then boyfriend didn't say anything. Thank God for friends. I made it home safe and immediately broke up with him. And yes, he pleaded and cried like someone had just told him his mother was dead."

He lives by her word.

Some men haven't realized what most of us accepted upon becoming adults—our parents taught us a lot, but they don't know everything. Whether a guy refuses to try sunny-side-up eggs because his mother only likes scrambled or won't shop at certain stores because his mom thinks they're "cheap," he clearly has a problem thinking for himself. The only thing more annoying than a boyfriend who tells you "I told you so" is one whose every sentence begins with "My mom says . . . ."

BIG RED-FLAG STORY:

"My ex was a staunch Republican because both of his parents were. He never read about the issues at hand (taxes, education, health care, etc.), he never researched candidates, and he sure as hell couldn't debate about any of these things. He sounded close-minded (and dumb) every time someone questioned his beliefs since he hadn't actually formed any."

He lives by her word . . . and expects you to do the same.

If your boyfriend not only lives by his mom's every edict but also expects you to play by her rules, we suggest you find a man secure enough to establish his own values and standards, or at least respect yours. One of our readers told us that a guy she once dated refused to let her sit at the bar in restaurants because his mom told him "Only sluts do that."

BIG RED-FLAG STORY:

"Sophomore year of college my roommate set me up with a guy from her soccer team. We made plans to see a movie that week-end, and I agreed to meet him at the theater since I lived nearby. When we got there, the movie was sold out, so I suggested we grab a coffee and see the later showing. To which he responded, 'That gets out after nine. My mom says good girls don't stay out that late and I don't want you to be uncomfortable.' The entire evening continued along those lines, him saying, 'My mom says good girls don't do this or that' to everything I suggested or said. I stuck it out, but told him after the movie I wasn't interested in dating him, and took the bus the three blocks home so he

wouldn't know where I lived. Shortly after I walked in the front
door, the phone rang and it was his mother, who proceeded to
scream at me for being a horrible person, telling me that I should
give her 'little boy' a second chance."

When his mother's rules take precedence over your freedom to do
whatever (and sit wherever) you want, you need to tell your guy
there's a new sheriff in town with her own set of laws. If he continues to push momma's morals on you, relinquish the relationship
before you find yourself questioning just who exactly runs your life.

THE BOTTOM LINE:
Momma's boys aren't necessarily bad guys. In fact, some of the
sweetest, kindest men we know are the biggest mother-lovers out
there. We, as women, recognize that there's a special bond between
mothers and sons that goes back to the womb. Then there are those
very special bonds between moms and sons that are sealed just a little
too tight. If your guy's a full-blown momma's boy you should know
he's a package deal.

When the duties of being a good son directly conflict with those of
being a good boyfriend, a momma's boy's loyalty will forever remain
with the woman who gave him life, not the one he supposedly wants
to spend his life with. Even if the hold his mom has on his life loos-
ens, she'll never let go completely. And he probably doesn't want
her to. Ask yourself whether you can swallow your pride and play
understudy or whether you need to be his leading lady. When back-
stage isn't where you want to be, find another dude because you'll
never be the headliner in a momma's boy's life.

TOP TEN RED FLAGS:

Questions He Asks on Your First Date

1. "Can I take a picture of you for my mom?"
2. "Do you wax your upper lip?"
3. "Can you promise you'll never cheat on me?"
4. "How wealthy are your parents?"
5. "Would you be interested in dating my cousin?"
6. "What's your ring size?"
7. "Do you watch *America's Most Wanted*?"
8. "Do you really think you should be eating that?"
9. "Are you one of those chicks who waits till the third date to have sex?"
10. "Could you do me a favor and wear more makeup next time?"

Chapter Seven

He Doesn't Know How to Communicate

You've probably heard it before, but we're going to tell you again: Effective communication is the key to a lasting relationship. The ability to bring up, discuss, and work through issues as they emerge is essential. So if your man rolls his eyes or pulls over to the side of the road and tells you to "get out," when you tell him you need to talk, chances are your relationship is on the skids.

Mature men should be able to express their feelings, ask for what they want, and receive constructive criticism—without screaming, whining, or pouting. Your man should also be capable of listening to what's on your mind without interjecting to correct or blame you. If he can't stand the heat and gets aggressive or, conversely, retreats into his shell, he doesn't understand what partnership is.

A WORD ON
Having a "Talk"

Most men wince when they hear the four dreaded words: "We need to talk." Once your boyfriend's on the defensive he's no longer listening to anything you say. Since you'd like him to hear what you have to say, we suggest being a little more strategic in your approach, by implementing what we call "the sandwich principle." Here's how it works: When you need to have a "talk" with your boyfriend, instead of immediately attacking him, begin the conversation by acknowledging something he does that totally works for you (piece of bread), to boost his ego a little bit. Then share whatever it is that's bothering you (meat), followed by something that you know will make him feel good (another piece of bread).

He'd rather type than talk.

Red-Flag Rule #12: If a guy can pick up a phone and send you a text, surely he can use the same phone and call you with it.

With e-mailing, texting, instant messaging, and Facebook, a true discussion has become easier than ever to avoid. We understand the inclination to hide behind electronics: It's easier to tell a gal something embarrassing, devastating, or risqué when you don't have to look her in the face. If your guy continually brings up serious relationship issues via IM, he's avoiding a real discussion.

BIG RED-FLAG STORY:

"My boyfriend told me he had an STD via Facebook message. Because he 'didn't want to discuss it' with me."

Not to mention that information shared via e-mail, IM, and text can be misconstrued, especially when just getting to know someone. Tone, doesn't translate well through these mediums, and can change the meaning of what's said, turning a sarcastic comment into a nasty remark. So, if this is your man's chosen means of communication, the two of you could end up spending more time second-guessing than getting to know each other.

He's a "pretty please"-er.

A man who can't properly communicate will whine about not getting his way or beg for you to give in. This immature behavior is selfish: He's hoping his pleading will outlive your patience. Which is likely. Watching a grown man grovel is most definitely not a turn-on, especially when he brings his pleading to the bedroom. Listen: If we say no, we mean no. And no matter how many times a guy pleads, "Come on baby, I really need this," we're not going to change our minds. Whether a guy begs you for sex, a back-rub, or a ride to his pal's place, he's clearly incapable of communicating like an adult.

When a two-year-old whines ceaselessly, the worst thing you can do is to give in and give him what he wants. Pacifying your man's pleading just encourages him to continue carrying on. If he knows you'll reward him for his irritating behavior, he has no reason to change it. Ignore your nagging nancypants until he realizes that his incessant pleas yield no response.

BIG RED-FLAG STORY:

"I ran into an ex-boyfriend a few years after we dated and we ended up back at his place. Before we even started kissing, he said, 'Give me a blowjob.' I said no. He said, 'Pleeeeeese,' in that annoying little kid whiny way. So, I did what I had to do: I waited for him to pass out, and escaped."

He overshares.

A good communicator can converse maturely and also knows what not to say. Some details are just too gross to share in order to preserve the romance. No girl wants to hear about her date having to "drop the kids off at the pool." (If that's the case, guys, just excuse yourself, do your thing, and we'll politely act as if we didn't notice.)

Then there are things that should strictly be kept on a need-to-know-basis. For example, we know a woman whose boyfriend is a deejay: On nights she doesn't go to the club, he almost always reports back about all of the girls hanging on his booth like he's giving out free Jell-O shots. Does she really need to know that? Now, if he were to hook up with one of the skanks, then that information would be something she needs to know. Since she doesn't think he's cheating, we assume he's telling her about the groupies in order to inflate his own ego, or, more likely, to deflate hers.

BIG RED-FLAG STORY:

"I don't know if it's a red flag, but it's probably not the best idea to tell the girl you potentially might hook up with that, in your experience, the majority of women out there don't know how to give good head and that it's a waste of time. Great incentive buddy, now I can't wait to suck your dick."

Other classic overshares include how many women he's slept with, the sexual acts he's done, the reasons he's cheated on exes, or his experience with two prostitutes in Amsterdam . . . yep, that happened to one of us. Along with paying for sex, not once but twice, Meagan's now ex-boyfriend also told her about the threesome he had with two bartenders at his previous job. Knowing this filthy feat left a bad taste in her mouth, making her feel dirty by association.

He undershares.

Most men aren't going to pour their hearts out and sob on your shoulder. They've been conditioned to believe that real men don't cry. And while your boyfriend isn't required to shed tears in front of you, it would be nice if he could clue you in as to what he's thinking every now and then.

If you've been dating your man for months, but you still haven't heard one mention of his childhood or career aspirations, something's not right. As the relationship builds, both of you should naturally divulge more personal information, creating a real bond with each other.

> *Red-Flag Rule #13:* If you're always the one doing all the sharing, it's time your man opens up and starts telling you something more substantial than the score of the game.

Just as there is certain information he shouldn't be sharing, there are details of his life that he must share because they affect you: his pending divorce, his history of herpes, or his addiction to crack, for example. When you have the feeling there's more to his story than what he's letting on, there usually is. Gently nudge your man to divulge by sharing something revealing about yourself.

BIG RED-FLAG STORY:

"A friend of my boyfriend's met a girl online and started dating her. Unfortunately for the girl, he'd purposely left off just a minor detail from his online profile, specifically that he was separated from his wife but not yet divorced. In fact, his profile claimed he'd never been married at all.

"After a couple of months, they started getting serious, and saying 'I love you' to each other, yet he still didn't tell her about his past—er, present, given that when his wife would call and text he'd lie and say it was one of his sisters. Of course, the relationship didn't work out because he dug himself a huge hole from the beginning. When he finally broke up with her, he didn't tell her that the real reason he needed to end the relationship was because he couldn't keep his lies going forever. And, naturally, the truth did come out after they broke up, like it always does."

He only pretends to listen.

If you're talking to your guy and his only response is "uh-huh, uh-huh," he's not paying attention, and he's most likely waiting for you to shut the hell up already. Conversing with some men is like talking to a bobblehead doll—they nod and nod, but never say anything. Or if they do utter a noise, it's likely a "sure" rather than a meaningful comment. If this sounds familiar, your man really isn't listening. He's planning his fantasy draft. Or his escape from the conversation.

You could tell him you're the kingpin of an ecstasy ring at the local high school or that you're headed to the Galapagos for a two-year study on sea turtle mating habits. A dude who doesn't listen clearly doesn't give a damn about what you have to say.

BIG RED-FLAG STORY:

"My husband has a listening problem. Let's say I spot him grabbing the milk from the fridge and drinking it straight from the carton. I'll tell him to please stop doing that and get a glass. He'll say okay. Then, minutes later, there he'll be drinking right from the carton again. When I call him out, he'll say I never told him not to do it. This will go on forever—he never actually respects my request. Sure, drinking from the carton isn't a huge deal, but he acts this way any time I ask him to do anything. It makes me wonder what other things I tell him that he's not actually listening to."

He avoids conflict.

Part of being an adult is dealing with conflict. We don't care if you and your boyfriend are a match made in heaven: No two people can carry on a relationship without encountering a dispute of some kind. So if you've been together for five years without a single argument, we'd be willing to bet it's not because you two always agree, but because either you or your significant other is adept at not actually verbalizing what's on your mind.

Men generally employ one of two strategies when trying to dodge a heavy discussion. Option one is to immediately apologize and agree with everything you say. A man who has no problem admitting he's made a mistake may seem like a dream come true, but he likely has no intention of actually changing his behavior. Empty apologies may dissolve the conflict, but they never solve the problem. Option two is to blow up and walk out, which doesn't resolve anything either.

Sure, the options above are better than screaming and punching walls, but whether your guy is a "yes man" or takes off to cool off and never comes back, he's still trying to sweep conflict under the rug . . . where it will accumulate dust only to re-emerge as a snarl-toothed bunny and eat you alive.

BIG RED-FLAG STORY:

"My best friend committed an enormous red flag: She got wasted one night and called her husband, who was at a bachelor party two states away, and demanded, screaming, that he come home on the next flight out. By the time he got home (later that night), she had sobered up and felt really bad about being such a bitch. She was prepared for a huge blow-out fight, or at least a discussion of why she flipped out. Instead, he walked in the door apologizing, saying that he shouldn't have gone to the party in the first place. Then he refused to talk about it and pretended nothing happened the next day."

He doesn't fight fair.

Whether it's because your guy's defensive or just a jerk, if he becomes excessively aggressive when the two of you have an argument, he isn't fighting fair—possibly the most detrimental trait of a bad communicator. Instead of dealing with the present, a boyfriend on the defense will often dig up the past, diverting the conversation away from him (which almost always means he knows he did something wrong).

A callous fighter often goes straight for the jugular, taking sharp jabs at your insecurities. You should never put up with your boyfriend attacking you on a personal level, which includes telling you "you're just like your mother," and, our favorite, calling you "crazy." As if he had nothing to do with making you emotional in the first place.

BIG RED-FLAG STORY:

"When my long-term boyfriend and I started dating in college, I made out with another guy one drunken night. It was a mistake and I felt bad so I came clean. This was literally the first month of what turned into a five-year relationship. For five years, he brought up this first-week make-out every time we fought. It was totally unfair and something he constantly used to guilt-trip me into getting his way."

THE BOTTOM LINE:

In a healthy relationship, both people should be heard and respected, whether they're debating who should win *American Idol* or discussing what's working (or not) in their relationship. Without proper communication nothing will ever get resolved, creating a build-up of resentment that will eventually explode all over you. (Yuck.)

We usually ignore communication problems in the early stages of a relationship when we're consumed by lust and excitement. But when those feelings fade and concerns arise, you need a guy who's considerate, compliant, and compassionate. So if your man has proven himself to completely lack the ability to discuss things with you like a mature adult, you can't really expect him to do the grunt work needed to sustain a mature relationship.

The road to true love is almost never smoothly paved. Since bumps and potholes are inevitable, it's best to find a guy who'll work through these obstacles with you, not make more of them.

TOP TEN RED FLAGS:
What He Does When You Fight

1. Asks "What—are you on your period?"
2. Asks "Are we breaking up?" and then starts crying
3. Leaves to go hang out with an ex-girlfriend
4. Tells you you're just like your mother
5. Calls his mother to bitch about you
6. Gets wasted instead of dealing with it
7. Makes faces and mimics you like a toddler
8. Reads off a laundry list of things he hates about you, going back to your first date
9. Throws, punches, or kicks various household items
10. Attempts to drown out your voice by turning the TV volume up

Chapter Eight

He Can't Take Care of Himself

On the road from child to adult, some guys stall out three-quarters of the way, never becoming self-sufficient. They don't clean, can't cook, and wouldn't know how to balance a checkbook if their lives depended on it. They've only gotten this far because someone—their mothers, sisters, or girlfriends (nudge, nudge)—have always been there to pick up their slack. These men are incapable of taking responsibility for their own lives; they expect others to act as their maids, chefs, and personal assistants.

A relationship should be a joint venture: two people who look out for each other, share responsibilities, and bring comparable portions of competency to the table. If you're holding up not just your end of the bargain but also a large load of his, you may build your triceps but you'll ultimately break your back. Constantly catering to your boyfriend's every whim leaves little time to address your own needs and emotions, which can eventually build bitterness toward your remiss Romeo.

The only relationship modeling most people receive is from their parents. So if your boyfriend went through childhood watching his mom do laundry, cook, and clean for the whole family while his dad watched the game with a beer, he's likely going to expect the same division of labor between the two of you. So unless you fantasize about serving hors d'oeuvres in an apron, heels, and pearls, you might want to chat with your indolent lad about your respective roles, specifically pointing out that he has one.

Of course, your dude may simply be lazy, immature, incompetent, or apathetic, in which case he needs to either shape up or ship out.

He's a sloppy Joe.

If he's nineteen, sleeping on a bed lofted by cinder blocks and surrounded by a sea of condom wrappers may seem normal. Once a guy's out of college, his pad shouldn't look like a frat house after a rush party. When your man's sink is covered in beard trimmings and you can't walk through his kitchen without sticking to the floor, you've got a sloppy Joe on your hands. Hopefully you've got strong thighs because you'll be squatting to pee for the entire length of the relationship.

A gross guy will likely expect you to adopt his low standards—don't be surprised if most nights consist of eating day-old pizza on his dirty-clothes-covered couch. A sloppy Joe is usually content in his filth and thinks you should be, too. Fight the urge to clean up after a begrimed boyfriend—he'll only get more reliant, transforming you from lover to mother.

A man who doesn't have the drive to take out the garbage or organize the pile of DVDs on his floor probably isn't motivated in other areas of his life, like his career or his relationship with you. How hard is it to clean the dishes in the sink or wipe down the bathroom counter when he knows you're swinging by? Your boy should take pride in his pad because he wants to impress you.

Red-Flag Rule #14: If there's mold growing in your guy's fridge, you should probably check the date on his condoms.

BIG RED-FLAG STORY:

"My ex-boyfriend's apartment was the messiest place I had ever seen. Every time he'd come home from wherever—school, a vacation, lunch—he'd simply dump whatever he had with him on his floor. Soon enough, his entire living room was carpeted in books, papers, clothes (dirty and clean), souvenirs, Christmas presents . . . you name it. And his bathroom was a whole other story: The floor was covered in little hairs from both his head and pubic region that he never bothered to sweep up, and his trashcan overflowed with tissues and Q-tips to the point that they spilled onto the floor.

"He started traveling a lot and the situation got so bad that you could barely walk through his place. Not knowing what else to do, I told him I wasn't going to sleep over until it was clean. He said he didn't have enough time, even though he spent roughly five hours a day watching TV."

A dude's heinous habits may extend beyond his home to his actual body. Less-than-stellar grooming and hygiene indicate that he doesn't value how others, including you, see him. He's not going to move forward in life (or in your relationship, we hope) smelling like he just scuba dove in a sewage dump. While it may seem superficial, your man's appearance is important both socially and professionally. He should care how he looks and smells because he wants you to be excited about getting up close and personal with him. If you'd rather stick your head in a gas station urinal than in his groin region, you need to re-evaluate whether you want to be with a guy who doesn't respect you enough to clean up his act.

WTF? *"In college, there was this guy I was pretty much in love with. One night he finally noticed me at a party and we went back to his place. In the dark, after a long make-out sesh, I knelt down to take his pants off. Much to my surprise, I was greeted by the worst smell known to man. I really liked him, and I didn't want to make him feel bad by leaving or telling him he stunk, so I excused myself, grabbed my travel-sized perfume bottle from my purse, coated my hands in fragrance, and proceeded to rub my nice-smelling hands all over his lower torso and thighs to counteract his stench. For the most part it worked. But after that hookup the guy's appeal was gone."*

He doesn't make his health a priority.

Men are infamous for avoiding medical care at all costs. While there are different theories as to why this is, most seem to revolve around the pressure society puts on men to appear tough. We understand that a dude doesn't want to be called a wuss, but there comes a point when seeing a doctor is unavoidable. The rash on his chest could be an allergy, but it could also be a symptom of something else, something more serious. And if he hasn't been to the doctor in ages, who knows what diseases, including sexual ones, he could have.

Plus, the longer he avoids getting treated, the longer you have to listen to his bitching. And you'll be frustrated by the fact that the one person he should be whining to (the doctor) is the one person he won't go to see.

BIG RED-FLAG STORY:

"My boyfriend shattered his hand while punching a guy from his soccer team in the back of the head. He went to the doctor and got a cast, but begged him to take it off a week early so he could go on a job interview without having to explain how he hurt himself. The doctor suggested physical therapy and gave him exercises to do every night. He neglected to do these and now, three months later, he complains that his hand hurts (mainly while playing video games). We end up getting in fights because he refuses to go back to the doctor or just start doing the damn exercises."

A man who's not taking care of himself in his twenties or thirties will only grow more obstinate over time, which is ironic because as men age, going to the doctor becomes increasingly important. If down the road your guy won't get a colonoscopy or prostate exam, you'll be the one worrying about him dying of undetected cancer. And you'll also be the one fighting with him every time he's due for a physical.

He participates in risky behavior.

It goes without saying that any man who abuses drugs and alcohol undervalues his health and his life. But keep in mind that he may in turn undervalue your life, not thinking twice before driving drunk or sleeping with you after shooting up with a dirty needle. (Of course, we don't condone dating a man with a heroin addiction in the first place.) When his life decisions affect your decision to live, you need get away from this dangerous dude.

BIG RED-FLAG STORY:

"This guy and I were driving down the Pacific Coast Highway on our first date when he asked me if I wanted a beer. I told him sure, thinking that we were going to stop at a bar and grab one. Nope. He reached behind my seat, pulled up a six-pack and gave me a beer. He also cracked one open for himself, which he proceeded to drink. While driving."

He can't complete routine adult tasks.

One of our blog readers told us that her twenty-three-year-old ex couldn't pack a suitcase—his mom had done it pre-college and his ex-girlfriend had done it during college. He expected someone else to plan his outfits, gather his toiletries, and even actually put the clothes in the bag, tasks that he apparently found too demanding.

Namby-pamby types like this guy have been overcoddled—they've always had someone to do their "to do" list items, so they never learned how to handle the most basic responsibilities of adult life, like filling out a job application, scheduling an appointment, or making sure not to overdraw their checking accounts.

Red-Flag Rule #15: If your boyfriend has acquired more than $385 in overdraft fees—in the span of two days—you probably don't want to combine your finances.

While those who enabled your man are partially to blame, the fact that he never tried to take ownership of these adult duties means that he's lazy. Whether he's too stoned to dial a phone or too stupid to set up recurring bill pay, he's banking on always having a girl to play secretary, and if you consent to this, you'll be led down a very slippery slope. Before you know it you'll be writing his thank-you notes, doing his taxes, and feeding him grapes off a vine. Any guy who loves and respects you wouldn't want to subject you to these very annoying responsibilities.

BIG RED-FLAG STORY:

"I dated this guy who would get hungry but not fix dinner until I got back home. He'd stay hungry for up to two days rather than pick up the phone and place a delivery order himself. I would get home at eleven P.M. and he'd ask if I could please order in for him because doing so himself was apparently too taxing. If I said I couldn't do it right away, he'd reply, 'Fine, I can stay like this for a little bit longer,' and then would keep bugging me that he was too hungry and I needed to do something about it."

He depends on you for every decision.

It's nice to feel like your man values your opinion—it shows that he respects your point of view, thinks you're pretty smart, and cares about how the decisions he makes may affect you.

But, if he calls from the dentist asking which toothbrush color he should choose or texts you for a Subway sandwich spread recommendation, his indecisiveness is not only aggravating but could also signal a lack of self-confidence and serious need for approval. While everyone gets by with a little help from their friends from time to time, if your incompetent beau doesn't have the self-assurance required to make small decisions—like what sweater to wear on Tuesday—you can't depend on him to help you make big ones.

BIG RED-FLAG STORY:

"Whenever my now-ex went on a business trip, he would call me constantly to help him make decisions. From what restaurant he should eat dinner at, to what he should actually order at dinner, to what blazer he should wear, he relied on me to pretty much tell him what to do, even when I was on the opposite coast."

THE BOTTOM LINE:

A guy who can't take care of himself inevitably becomes overly reliant on someone, most often his certain someone, a.k.a. you, adding stress to your day-to-day life. Resist your caretaking instincts and force this man to learn to live on his own or you'll start to feel more like his servant than his sweetheart.

No matter how charming, handsome, or book smart a guy is, if he can't handle do-it-himself skills, he's not ripe for the picking. Managing his life will take over yours, and you may eventually have to choose between his livelihood and your own. If you miss the dermatologist appointment you waited a month to get because you're busy arguing with your beau's building manager for a lower rent, his minor priorities are taking precedence over your major ones, creating a lopsided relationship that's detrimental to your physical and emotional health. Besides, who wants to have sex with a man who hasn't cleaned under his fingernails since the Clinton administration anyway?

TOP TEN RED FLAGS:
Things You Find in His Fridge

1. Mold
2. His ex-girlfriend's Nuvaring
3. A shriveled carrot that looks like a shrunken penis
4. Half a ham from Christmas 2005
5. Nothing—there is literally not a thing in the fridge
6. Roaches
7. A puddle of unidentifiable green goop
8. His wisdom teeth
9. A half-eaten McDonald's hamburger
10. Sperm samples

A GUY WITHOUT A REAL SENSE of adult identity will never be able to develop a deep bond with you—he doesn't have the confidence or competence to do so. We say it's time to get a little selfish: Pay less attention to his bullshit and more to your own shit (figuratively, of course). Then tell him to grow up or get lost—if he's unwilling to clean his sheets, break from his mother's grip, or learn to communicate constructively, you should be unwilling to continue with the relationship.

There are plenty of bigger, stronger, sexier fish in the dating sea, so why not throw on a cute bikini, hop back in the water, and find yourself a man capable of swimming without floaties.

Red-Flag Case Study #2

See how many red flags you can spot in just one story:

I was on vacation with my boyfriend and his family in Nantucket when all of us—his mom, dad, brother, him, and me—decided to head to the beach. When we got there, it was freezing. Still, my boyfriend immediately wanted to jump in the water, and he wanted me to go with him. I said I was way too cold, but I figured we could compromise: he'd swim in the water, and I'd walk along the shore, so we could still hang out or whatever. This was unacceptable. He warned me that if I didn't come in the water he was going to be mad at me and not speak to me for the rest of the day. I figured he was being a little overdramatic and, since I don't respond well to threats, I stayed on my towel with the rest of the group while he went in the water. When he came back from swimming, I asked him how it was, and, as promised, he gave me the silent treatment.🚩 His mom asked him why he was being so rude to me and he muttered that it was because I wouldn't go swimming.🚩 She tried to help the situation by telling him he needed to snap out of his bad mood. He just shrugged.🚩 Then his brother tried to reason with him.🚩 Embarrassed, I pretended to read a magazine so no one knew I was crying. He knew I was upset but ignored me for the rest of the time we were at the beach.🚩 Later he sort of apologized when we were all back at his family's house—but it was mainly because his mother made him.🚩

🚩 He uses threats to get what he wants. That's never acceptable.

🚩 The silent treatment? Wow. Really?

🚩 He's treating her so badly that his mom notices.

🚩 He's spoiled and disrespectful.

🚩 He's a total baby. Why does his whole family have to tell him how to treat his girlfriend? We're guessing they're used to this behavior.

🚩 He just doesn't give a shit that he made his girlfriend cry.

🚩 He's not genuine. His "sorry" is more of an appeasement than a true apology.

Part Three

He's a Freak in Bed . . . and Not in a Good Way

Chapter Nine
He's Bad in Bed

We would be thrilled if every guy was a pro in the fornication field. But if you've had a few bedmates, it's likely that at least one of them was bad in the sack. From the sloppy kisser to the foreplay forgoer to the one-minute man, your lover obviously isn't revving your engine if you're thinking "I'd rather be at the DMV right now" while having sex.

> *Red-Flag Rule #16:* If a guy has to ask how many times you came, chances are you didn't.

Bad-in-bed behavior usually depends less on experience and more on a guy's attitude and degree of attention. A novice who takes direction and seeks to please is better than a Lothario who focuses only on his enjoyment and blows you off when you tell him how to get you off. Even though guys can improve in bed if they want to, having to train a thirty-year-old man who, excuse our French, fucks like a frat boy, is tedious. If you're going to give a crash course on female pleasure, you may as well find a young buck who can go five rounds a night.

While sex isn't everything in a relationship, it's certainly an integral part of the bond you share with your beau. When you don't want to have sex with your man because he's a sap in the sack, you may suffer from the loss of intimacy. Your disinterest in seeing him naked may progress to a disinterest in seeing him altogether.

He's just clueless.

A man who requires a map to find your clit or focuses solely on the obvious erogenous zones definitely didn't pay attention in health class and hasn't bothered to familiarize himself with the female physique since. While there are some things dudes will always find confusing about our anatomy, they could just do a little research and have the basics covered.

> *Red-Flag Rule #17:* If he mashes your lady parts like he's kneading pizza dough, tell him to lighten up before you're too swollen to cross your legs.

BIG RED-FLAG STORY:

"I was finally hooking up with this guy I had liked for a long time. We were making out on my couch when he suddenly tapped my cheek until I stopped kissing him. He guided my chin down to part my lips a little more and then he stuck his tongue on my gums and proceeded to lick the inner rim of my lips, in a circle, all the way around my mouth. I didn't know what to do so I just kept making out with him. But then, when he tapped my cheek to try to mouth-rape me again, I pulled away from him, realizing that was likely his signature 'move.' I told him I had to get to bed and kicked him out of my place. We never made out again."

As Julie well knows, a guy who can't discern labia from leg will never be able to satisfy you in bed. She semi-dated a guy who humped her leg repeatedly—while awake, sober, and clothed. He clearly hadn't hooked up with many girls, and apparently never watched an R-rated movie because he seemed to think her vagina was on her left thigh or that her left thigh had a serious number of nerve endings.

He doesn't understand foreplay.

Although a woman's need to warm up before the big game is well documented, some men's idea of foreplay is asking, "Do you have lube?" (This is ironic because if they actually spent a little time touching, kissing, licking, etc., we'd naturally produce some for them.) Of course, using lube to speed things up is fine, but if your bedfellow doesn't know how to arouse you, he may see sex as a solo act with a vagina instead of a two-person undertaking with a woman.

BIG RED-FLAG STORY:
"I'd been lusting after this guy for months, and we soon started hooking up. The only problem was that his way of trying to pleasure me was to just forcefully jam his fingers inside me. I wish I could say that I stopped hooking up with the guy, but I was super attracted to him and just thought his skills would get better over time. Nope. I gave him blowjobs and he basically kept doing the 'Stayin' Alive' dance into my vagina."

Make your need for an appetizer before the meal known. And if he's doing a subpar job, casually and carefully (men's egos are fragile) mention or show him something you like. Generally, once a guy sees a gal get off from his handiwork, he's more than willing to repeat the foreplay feat. If he completely ignores your requests and keeps at his wham-bam-thank-you-ma'am pace, he's a selfish, careless, and flat-out bad lover whom you should bed no more.

He's lazy in bed.

A laggard guy always positions you on top so he can lie there while you do all the work or pass out after you give him head so he doesn't have to reciprocate. Sure, it may require some effort to get a gal off, but if you continually ask your man to go down on you and in response he sighs and gives a half-hearted "fine," he's officially lazy in bed. And we hate to say it, but if your man isn't proactive in bed, he may be the type who expects everyone else, especially you, to pick up his slack in other areas of his life.

BIG RED-FLAG STORY:
"When my ex-boyfriend bought a vibrator for me, I was kind of excited to spice things up. However, a few drunken nights later, he inadvertently revealed that he hadn't gotten the toy to please me, he'd gotten it because he was so lazy that he didn't want to 'do any sexual work' anymore."

A lazy guy is far worse than a clueless one: This dude actually knows what he's supposed to do but chooses the easy route anyway. A man who's unwilling to work a little to please you a lot will never be the type to work a lot to please you a little, both in and out of the bedroom. And since we all know it's the small things a guy does that count the most, a lazy lover isn't worth your TLC.

He can't communicate in bed.

A man's ability to take verbal or physical cues will make or break him in bed. A guy who can't communicate will either ignore or misinterpret your in-bed requests. You'll ask him to lighten his touch and he'll stop touching you altogether. He'll ask "You like that? You like that?" but it doesn't matter if you don't because he's not waiting for an answer . . . he's just gonna keep on thrustin' on until he gets himself off, instead of responding to the feedback your body, or your mouth, is giving him.

Communication issues are not limited to when you're actually having sex. How a man lets you know he's in the mood is also telling. "Come on baby, I need you to help keep the jizz off my mind" (actual quote) is not the way he should convince you to drop trough. And no matter how much a gal enjoys a blowjob, no one appreciates a heavy hand urging her head down. We're all for receiving a little instruction and men should be able to verbalize what they want in bed, but beware of the dude whose way of suggesting a new position is not to use his voice.

BIG RED-FLAG STORY:

"Right before this guy and I had sex, we'd be making out, him on top, and, all of a sudden, he would crawl up so his knees were on either side of my shoulders and stick his dick in my face, expecting me to suck it. There were no words, no 'Hey, could you do that thing I like so much?' Just his penis in my freakin' face."

His dirty talk is just too dirty.

Sure, most women enjoy a little erotic language but there's a distinction between subtly sexy and downright dirty. Your guy whispering "I can't wait to get you home" in your ear is far different from him proclaiming "I can't wait to stick my dick in your mouth." When language intended to loosen you up makes you cringe, it's a sign that he has no clue what turns a woman on, especially you. That's a problem.

If a guy refuses to decrease the dirty talk, it's probably because he's using it to turn himself on and not you—a sign of a selfish lover.

> *Red-Flag Rule #18:* A man should never use the word "pussy" while he's in yours.

BIG RED-FLAG STORY:

"My friend hooked up with a guy we called 'the dirty talker.' He tended to say things that turned her off, instead of on. For example, they'd be having sex and instead of 'This feels good' or 'I like how you feel,' he'd say, 'Your tightness makes my cock throb.' Even though he was normal in most other ways, she couldn't look at him without hearing his (un)sexy talk in her head."

He thinks sex is a performance.

Most women don't enjoy being treated like a porn star. If your name's not Bunny and you're not the leading lady in *The Lord of the Cockrings*, your guy shouldn't attempt to recreate a XXX scene in your bedroom. If he jizzes on your face or slaps it with his dick, other than making you feel objectified and uncomfortable, he's confusing porn sex with real sex.

BIG RED-FLAG STORY:

"Every time I hooked up with this guy I was dating, he would flip me around on my knees for doggie style. Which was fine, except that, after the first couple of times, I realized that he liked that position so he could watch himself rail me in his closet mirrors. He pretty much forgot I was there because he was too busy getting off on his own performance."

Treating sex like a one-man show devalues an emotional experience. Your dude should be concentrating on your enjoyment. We'd certainly rather look bad and feel good between the sheets than vice versa. A porntastic performer who focuses on the mirror instead of your eyes isn't concerned with bonding, only boning.

He has bad after-sex etiquette.

How a guy treats you right after sex can be just as important as how he treats you during it. We addressed men who treat women like sluts in Chapter 2, but there are plenty of other wrong moves a dude can make during those first few minutes after sex. Turning on SportsCenter, checking his e-mail, or simply saying something irrelevant, like "I think I'm going to buy a water purifier," after he was just inside you is off-putting to say the least.

WTF? *"When it was time for bed, whether we'd been fighting or just had sex, my ex would stuff a pillow between us so that I couldn't touch him during the night."*

Most men know sex is emotional for women and that we tend to feel particularly vulnerable during those just-after moments. So, when he's busy doing something else instead of holding you for some after-sex spooning, it's easy to feel used. His behavior may not be intentional, but it's still inconsiderate and hurtful. How hard is it to simply hold your gal for three minutes? A guy should respect your need for, in the words of Michael Bolton, a little time, love, and tenderness.

BIG RED-FLAG STORY:
"My boyfriend and I were lying in bed less than five minutes post-sex, still sweaty, still naked, when he reached for his phone

saying that he had to ask his uncle a question about an upcoming family vacation, which was three months away. When the call went to his uncle's voicemail, he dialed his grandma. When grandma didn't pick up, he called his brother, who also didn't answer. Now, I'm not the type of gal who needs an hour of cuddling, but come on. There is a time and a place for calling family members and, unless there's an emergency, that time and place is not in your bed when I'm lying there next to you naked."

THE BOTTOM LINE:

You can excuse a guy for being bad in bed, but if he's too proud to ask for direction or too self-serving to tend to your needs, and as a result makes you unhappy, we suggest you find a new bedmate. Bad sex is inevitable from time to time, but bad sex all the time is a downright crime. While he may be the offender, you don't have to be his victim.

TOP TEN RED FLAGS:
T-Shirt Slogans We've (Unfortunately) Seen

1. FBI: Female Body Inspector
2. The Man [arrow pointing up], The Legend [arrow pointing down]
3. It isn't going to lick itself!
4. Cougar Bait
5. Orgasm Donor
6. Vagina is for Lovers
7. Ass: The Other Vagina
8. Vagitarian
9. I Support Single Moms [with a graphic of a stripper on a pole]
10. Ask Me About Our Blowjobs for Drinks Program

Chapter Ten

He's Weird in Bed

Even if you're dating a total gentleman, when the time comes to do the dippity-doo-da you may discover that he has some rather unusual sexual desires. In fact, you may be in a relationship for months, even years, thinking your guy is destined to be the father of your child, when all of sudden he says he'd like to wear your panties and be spanked with a studded leather whip. Happens every day, ladies. Happens. Every. Day.

Just like there's a whole spectrum of sexuality, there's a wide variety of what people actually like to do in bed. Visit a sex shop and you'll find ball gags and nipple clamps that make the average vibrator and handcuffs seem vanilla. There are online communities and clubs dedicated to every sexual fetish—from feet to robots. But the toy or club of choice isn't really the issue here. When it comes to sex, it's all about how you feel about what, and whom, you're doing.

Your comfort, as the phrase goes, is key. If your boyfriend wants to engage in a sexual activity that you're not okay with, say so. A stand-up guy will respect the fact that you're not ready to go there with him, possibly ever. A not-so-great guy will try to convince you that it's your duty to indulge his every fantasy. It's not. If a dude pressures you to do something you clearly tell him you don't want to do, he's a jerk. Plain and simple. (More on this in Chapter 11.)

> *Red-Flag Rule #19:* If a guy turns you for doggie style within the first couple of times you sleep together, don't be surprised when he tries to stick it in your ass soon after.

With that in mind, here are some of the signs that your guy isn't just a little freaky, but a full-on freak. Remember: The sex acts themselves are not the Big Red Flags here per se (although some of them may not be your thing); what matters most is the way a guy treats you in conjunction with these acts and how his participation in them affects you.

He doesn't want to get off . . . or can't.

We touched on this briefly in Chapter 4: There's something just plain weird about a straight man who doesn't want to be touched by his willing-to-please girlfriend. Sure, guys can be tired, upset, or not in the mood. But if your guy is only game for getting you off, and doesn't want you to reciprocate, it's a red flag that shouldn't be ignored and could even indicate a medical or psychological problem. Something is definitely up, if his member isn't.

BIG RED-FLAG STORY:

"I met this guy a couple of weeks ago at a party thrown by some mutual friends. He's gorgeous, funny, and all of our friends vouch for him. All signs say he's into me. We've made out dozens of times by now and he's invited me over to his place twice. Both times I've tried to go down on him, but he says he's 'tired' and won't let me. The weird thing is he's very insistent on returning the favor I haven't given him yet, and has gotten me off both times. He's had sex with previous girlfriends before—so what's the deal?"

It's easy to feel inadequate or confused when a man doesn't want to have sex with you or won't allow you to venture south. (Come on, what guy turns down a blowjob?) You may begin to wonder if he's holding off because you're a failure at fornicating or because he's trying to hide a herpes outbreak. Every scenario possible will run through your head as you ponder why he wants to be with you if he doesn't want to sleep with you, driving you to the brink of insanity.

His porn habit is ruining your sex habit.

Ah, porn. It's a topic that's been debated by feminists for years: Is it misogynistic, portraying women as sex objects? Or is it empowering for women to showcase their sexuality, and make some cash while doing so? We're not really gonna go there except to say that, for the most part, we don't think porn in itself is a big deal. (Unless it's the kiddie or barely legal variety. In that case, you must run. Fast.) Men are visual creatures and get off on watching other people have sex. So do a lot of women.

That said, it's totally natural to feel a little self-conscious if your guy has a penchant for porn and to wonder why he's fantasizing about a girl who's onscreen when he could have, or even currently has, one in his bed. If, like most women, you have normal-size breasts, cellulite, and pubic hair that isn't styled to look like a Playboy bunny, you may begin to doubt your sex appeal. Plus, unless you've mastered theatrical moaning and have a double-jointed pelvis, you may be intimidated by the moves your movie buff may expect in the bedroom.

Think about how, when, and why your guy uses cinematic stimulation. A dude who stays up all night cruising XXX sites and is too tired to go to work the next day clearly has a problem with porn. If he spends more time watching porn than trying to get in your panties, he's probably an addict who needs porn to get off, whether he's by himself or you're naked with him. When he has an unhealthy relationship with sex, he shouldn't be in a relationship with you. Instead, he should attend a support group to work on his fixation with filmic fantasies.

BIG RED-FLAG STORY:

"My guy really liked watching porn, which wasn't my thing but I was okay with it. However, he liked having it on while we were getting it on, which upset me because he'd just watch the screen instead of looking at me. He said he'd try to have sex without the porn on in the background but when we shut it off, he couldn't get it up."

His activities behind closed doors are just not okay.

Everyone needs some alone time to regroup and tend to their personal business like catching up on phone calls, paying bills, reading cheesy celebrity magazines, and whatnot. Many men use their personal moments to rub one out. Some guys have super-high sex drives and need to masturbate once a day; others can get by yanking it every now and then during dry spells. Such behavior is healthy and even has a biological imperative: Masturbating lets men release built-up sexual fluid and this keeps their sperm in good condition so they can later fertilize us with it.

Masturbation is a bit like porn. Problems occur when a guy's solo sex affects your coupled sex: for example, if he can't get off during intercourse and needs to jack off after, if he masturbates to the point of penis pain, or if he turns down sex because his chronic stroking habit has left him too spent to get it up.

It may be more than masturbating that has him tuckered out. The Internet has made virtual cheating as easy as a click of the mouse. Any dude can find a girl willing to sex chat or strip in front of a webcam. If your man spends hours ordering a college coed to bend over and grab her ankles, he may not be cheating in the traditional sense, but he's definitely doing something dirty that will negatively impact your real-life relationship.

BIG RED-FLAG STORY:

"I've been dating a guy for over two years. Let me start by saying that, throughout the entire time I've known him, he's been the best thing to ever happen to me. He's beautiful, always manages to make me laugh, has a great job, wonderful family, and my family loves him. Not to mention, the sex is mind-blowing and he loves going down on me (and is phenomenal at it). So, what could be the problem, you ask? Let me back it up a little . . .

"When we first started dating, I was drawn to the fact that he was smart and a gentleman. After a few dates and naughty texts, he offered to send me naked pictures of himself via cell phone. He seemed pretty eager to do so, and I was curious, so I accepted.

"Fast forward to present time: 'Mr. Perfect' told me he had something guilty weighing on his conscience. He told me that he has a habit of seducing out-of-state women on various webcam chat sites, then pleasuring himself in front of them (still on webcam). He said, when he was single, he used to do it all the time, displaying almost addictive behavior. Disgusted, I asked him why, and he responded that he equated it to porn, but it was interactive and challenging. He also said he relished the compliments he received from the girls about his huge manhood, which is weird because he never seemed insecure.

"The worst part is that he admitted to having done this a few times since we've been together. He asserts that he always feels pathetic and ashamed afterward, and he has since thrown away his webcam and changed his passwords to those websites to something he can't remember in order to avoid temptation.

"I love this guy with all of my heart, and I'm so upset he marred my image of him. He insists that it was just an erotic game to him, but I still feel betrayed. I guess the red flag here was when he wanted to expose himself to me: If a man is that enthusiastic about showing you photos of himself naked, he's probably eager to do it for others."

He's a cross-dresser.

While you may not be able to picture a meaty hunk of a man in a corset, we swear there are guys out there who strut around in lingerie. However, a guy who dons lady clothes doesn't necessarily have a penchant for penises. He may just like the feel of silk panties.

Still, learning that your manly, beer-guzzling guy exhibits very feminine behavior may make you feel like he's been putting on a front, tricking you into thinking he's something he's not. Cross-dressing reverses the normal roles men and women play, which can be confusing and create insecurity regarding your own femininity.

BIG RED-FLAG STORY:
"I started dating a guy who seemed very manly. Then, two weeks into the relationship he asked if I would be okay with

him wearing some women's clothes in bed. Sure . . . whatever you like, I said. It started with a silk tank. A few weeks later we went on a weekend trip and I came out of the bathroom to find him standing there in a wig and a full-length black-lace getup. While the full ensemble shocked me, the worst part was his hideous black Payless pumps. If you're going to cross-dress, for the love of God, at least do it with some style. That was the last time we had sex. But I did help him shop for some better shoes so he'd be ready for the next girl."

Some men think cross-dressing is a harmless expression of attributes they're told by society to hide and others feel shameful about their taboo tendencies. So, even if you're okay with your dude playing dress-up, he may have some psychological issues regarding identity that could impact your relationship in other ways. Seriously consider whether you're committed enough to your man, and confident enough in your own sexuality, to proceed with this atypical relationship.

A WORD ON
Europeans

Imagine: He's older, he's sexy, and he's swooned you into his bed. Lights out, candles lit, clothes off, game on. But wait . . . is he wearing panties? If you hook up with a foreign man, the answer sometimes is yes. We're not talking about tightie-whities here, but French-cut manties. And while they may seem a little odd, and perhaps a bit ladylike to you, manties are perfectly normal underwear-fare for European men.

He's into some freaky shit.

In one of our blog submissions, a girl told us she once dated a guy who had a sex locker filled with five types of lube, several sets of handcuffs, and a bunch of vibrating cock rings. If you're not used to seeing these sort of items, doing so is quite surprising, even unnerving. If and when you're comfortable, we suggest asking your guy to describe his fantasies or show you what his toys do. Discussing what turns him on will more often than not turn you on, and you'll be going at it like fluffy little bunnies in no time. But, like everything else, there is a line: Only you know what you're comfortable talking about and exploring. Sometimes, the line between kinky and full-on freaky is quite thin.

BIG RED-FLAG STORY:

"At the beginning of a new relationship, I went to my guy's house for drinks and a movie. At some point, I had to pee so I asked him to pause the DVD player. He said he would and offered to make us another cocktail while I went to the bathroom. After doing my thing, I opened the door to exit the bathroom and found him crouching next to the door. Confused, I asked him what he was doing. He said, 'Oh. I like to listen to girls pee. I think it's fun.' Umm, okay. It didn't seem like a huge red flag at the time, but it was the first of many that were about to come."

He's into some freaky shit . . . and he keeps it from you.

Sex is essential to a romantic relationship. So is communication. Put them together and you're likely to have a functioning, healthy bond. One without the other, not so much. If your guy keeps his kinky tendencies secret, whatever freaky shit he's doing isn't the problem—the fact that he isn't being honest with you, or perhaps feels like he can't be, is.

BIG RED-FLAG STORY:

"I had just moved from my hometown to the opposite coast and my boyfriend and I decided to keep our over-a-year-long relationship going despite the distance. About six months after I moved, he called to say he had something to tell me. I braced myself, thinking he had cheated on me. He revealed to me that, a couple of months earlier, he'd apparently purchased anal beads and a butt-plug. He'd been using them. On himself. By himself. Although there wasn't another girl involved, I still felt cheated on, wondering not only why he was using anal beads to masturbate, but also why he had kept it a secret that he later felt he needed to confess."

A WORD ON
Anal Play

In Chapter 4 we discussed some of the red flags that indicate your man may like men. We left out anal play because the prostate is an erogenous zone that both straight and gay men alike may derive pleasure from. However, if your guy constantly requests to do you in the ass—or he wants you to do him in the butt with a strap-on—it's pretty hard not to suspect that he'd prefer a penis to your vagina. While there's nothing wrong with your guy if he's anally inclined, be honest with yourself about whether or not you're prepared to deal with the after-the-fact consequences of indulging in his backdoor fantasies, which can range from feeling a little weirded out to not being physically attracted to him anymore.

While seeing a sex locker on date three may be disturbing, finding out about your dude's freakiness a year into a serious relationship leaves you with a tougher decision because serious emotions are involved. Although you may feel betrayed, keeping his behavior a secret could have nothing to do with you: He may have a long-standing problem that he's ashamed to admit. Or maybe he anticipates that you're not open-minded enough to accept anything outside the lovemaking norm. If you are in fact uncomfortable venturing into the world of deviant sex, accept that the two of you operate on different sexual wavelengths and go find a fella on your frequency.

He's into some freaky shit . . . and he tries it out on you without asking.

We don't even know what to say about this one. Perhaps because it goes *without* saying that a guy shouldn't sneak-attack you with the freaky stuff he fancies. Whether he's got a rogue finger lingering near your backdoor, takes a Taser to your titty, or decides to surprise-handcuff you to the bed, this rather creepazoid behavior both disrespects you and puts your trust in him at risk.

> *Red-Flag Rule #20:* A guy should never whip out his ex-girlfriend's vibrator to use on you. There are just some things that should be purchased anew.

BIG RED-FLAG STORY:

"I was taking a shower with my now ex-boyfriend when all of a sudden he informed me that he'd peed on me, just to 'see what it would be like.' Then he tried to backpedal saying it was simply 'easier' than to use the toilet, which was two feet away. Maybe he could have asked me if I minded. Instead, he peed on me and then told me he did it."

THE BOTTOM LINE:

It's important to know what you are comfortable with sexually and what you aren't, and frankly, the only way to know for sure is to either seriously consider how you feel about it or try it. That said, if you do end up experimenting with your man, please know that you aren't required to repeat the erotic activities again, nor are you opening the floodgates for all kinds of perverse panty play. Also remember that men have fragile egos, so don't berate a guy for being into some crazy shit if he happens to share his affinity for le freak with you and it just ain't your bag, baby.

Sex is important—it's what separates friends from lovers. So if you're not loving the fact that your man enjoys sticking a plug up his ass, it's time to get your sweet little ass out of that relationship.

TOP TEN RED FLAGS:
Things He Collects

1. Signed Hooters coasters
2. STDs
3. Women's panties
4. Porn-site passwords
5. VIP wristbands from Spring Break '98
6. Ed Hardy T-shirts
7. Taxidermies
8. Marijuana roaches
9. Used condoms
10. Erotic poetry

Chapter Eleven

He's Mean in Bed

You may know the words to every song on Snoop Dogg's *Doggie Style* album, but is "Suck my dick, bitch" something you really want to hear while being intimate with your lover? We certainly don't think so. And we'd hope you wouldn't put up with such blatant disrespect.

Bad bedroom etiquette is one thing—a guy who makes you feel insecure or uncomfortable when you're having sex with him is another. Whether he's too aggressive, disrespectful, or chauvinistic, or coerces you into doing things you don't want to do, he has forgotten one thing: Having sex with you is a privilege. And not one he should abuse. If he ever wants to get lucky again, that is.

> *Red-Flag Rule #21:* A guy should never say "It's all in your head" when you tell him that you need to stop during sex because it hurts.

If your boyfriend, lover, or bed buddy is committing any of the following red flags, we suggest ditching him all together.

He's pushy with his poker.

Like proud peacocks, some men flaunt their he-cocks like glorious feathers. As long as Rod doesn't flash his Johnson to unsuspecting bystanders or children, we're generally fine with it. But the moment a man starts shoving his dick anywhere near our faces, we're liable to bite it off.

BIG RED-FLAG STORY:

"I once lived with a guy who stuck his dick in my face whenever he felt like it. Whether I was working at my desk or watching TV, if my mouth was crotch level, you can bet his penis would be there prodding to get in. Even if I told him I didn't want to (or couldn't) give him head, he would stand there waiting—hips thrust forward—just in case I accidentally turned my head."

There's nothing wrong with a man making sexual requests, as long as he's clear that they are indeed requests—not requirements. Any guy who acts like he deserves to dip into your honey pot whenever his stick gets dry doesn't respect your right to say no. Ladies, we are the keepers of our coochies; please don't let men think otherwise.

WTF? *"A boyfriend once told me that he made his ex-girlfriend suck his dick every time they had sex. (They dated for two years, mind you.) His reason for sharing this? It was a testament of his love for me since he didn't make me do that."*

He's not just demanding, he's downright forceful.

Whether a man phrases his desires as questions or orders speaks volumes about him. In the equation of love all partners should be considered equal, and the master/servant scenario should fall under role-play only. The moment your man starts ordering you around or pressuring you into sex, you should put the lock down on your chastity belt and swallow the key. The bedroom should be neutral territory, where control is shared evenly.

> *Red-Flag Rule* #22: If he accuses you of being "sexually repressed" when you tell him that joking about rape isn't funny, he probably doesn't abide by the "no means no" rule.

BIG RED-FLAG STORY:

"I had just gotten out of a really nasty relationship and rebounded with a guy who, at first, seemed really nice. But, he steadily became more and more demanding. When I'd say 'no' to sex he'd plead and then end up pressuring, even ordering, me into it. It was okay at first, because I kind of like the whole dominance/submission bit, but sometimes 'no' really means 'no' and he didn't seem to get that.

"Eventually, I had to go back to college. To help with the long-distance relationship, he asked me to take pornographic pictures and videos of myself to send to him. Fearing they'd get stolen and somehow posted somewhere public, I said I wouldn't do it. He got angry and then told me this shocker: He'd taped us having sex without my knowledge or consent, and if I didn't deliver on the photos and videos, he'd post our intimate moments online, essentially ruining my life.

"Well, I broke up with him, and while I'm probably on some website now, it was well worth it to be free of that creep."

Even if you're into the S&M scene, you should still be able to set boundaries without worrying about your man breaking them. We don't care if you're decked out in latex with a choker and chain around your neck, you still have the right to decide when and where you become submissive.

He guilts you into playing along.

Red-Flag Rule #23: When your boyfriend agrees not to break up with you as long as you consent to anal sex, where does his guilting stop?

Just because your boyfriend tries to convince you that the majority of women are fine with—even turned on by—having, let's say, a beer bottle shoved up their birth canal, it doesn't mean you're inferior or inadequate, or even prudish, if you don't. If you've told your boyfriend you aren't comfortable doing something specific under the sheets, he shouldn't want you to do it. End of story. He also shouldn't compare what you won't do with what his last girlfriend actually did.

Then there's the "come-on-baby-do-it-for-me" card. As long as the request isn't too far outside your comfort zone, sure, you may be willing to try things that you're not particularly interested in to please your man. But when a guy's wants extend beyond what you're capable of rationalizing, and he demands you do them anyway, you need to get dressed and exit immediately before he forces you to do something that'll give you that dirty, creepy feeling because you only half consented. If he ever makes you feel as though there's something wrong with you for not wanting to play along, he's an asshole.

BIG RED-FLAG STORY:

"My boyfriend really wanted to have anal sex with me, and I really didn't want to do it, so, to keep him from pressuring me, I told him that if he ever whisked me away to Hawaii (as he'd told me he wanted to do at some point in our relationship), I would do it then. (Not exactly smart, but it was the only way I could get him to shut up about it.)

"When our two-year anniversary came along, he got a really nice hotel room for us. When I got there, I saw that he'd decorated the entire place: There were leis, grass skirts, a coconut bra, and water bottles in the shape of pineapples. He told me that since we couldn't actually go to Hawaii right then, he'd recreated it for me—not as some nice romantic gesture, of course, but so I would have anal with him.

"After fighting about it for a bit, I agreed to let him just do it. It was our anniversary; he'd spent like $500 on the hotel room; I was sick of arguing about it; blah blah blah. After he got it in like an inch, I was horrified and uncomfortable and told him to stop. He did, but for the rest of our relationship (which lasted longer than I can admit without being embarrassed), he'd harass me about doing it again—since it didn't go in all the way, he said it 'didn't count.'"

He's mind-fucking you.

Your guy may not use physical force, but will instead flex his dominance by mentally tossing you around the bedroom. If he's in complete control of when and where and in what position you do the dirty—his game isn't kinky, it's full-on manipulative.

One of Meagan's ex-boyfriends wasn't the nicest guy, and she'd have to schedule sex with him. During one of these not-so-passionate appointments, she went to kiss him and he pulled away, telling her, "You didn't say anything about kissing." He wouldn't make out with her because she didn't ask, but sex was fine because she had gotten permission.

BIG RED-FLAG STORY:

"Lying naked in bed one morning I told my new guy that I was really, really in the mood to have sex. He refused. Ego bruised, I started to get dressed and just as I was pulling my pants on he started taking them off, kissing the back of my neck. Excited I was going to get laid, I went with it. It didn't occur to me until later that he basically turned me down, enjoyed watching me become uncomfortable and then had his way with me when I least expected it, which in the end was more demeaning than enjoyable."

Manipulation, unlike demands or force, can be as subtle as your man is smooth. These men are good at their game, and you're typically left questioning how you (the strong, assured woman you are) ended up so subservient. But when you're lying there naked, with all your flaws exposed, it's easy for manipulative men to break down your self-confidence. (We'll discuss this more in Chapter 16.)

A little comment here and there about the size of your butt, or a few snide remarks about liking girls with bigger breasts (implying bigger than yours), and soon enough a guy can transform you into an insecure chick—and have you convinced that you're totally undesirable to every other man except, of course, him. (*He'll* have sex with you. Aren't you lucky?)

He has zero concern for your sexual safety.

Fun and games aside, sex is a serious matter and comes with consequences that shouldn't be taken lightly. Men will never know the hell of missing a period: They will never beg the menstrual gods for the tiniest drop of blood on their panties, and they will never spend the longest ten minutes of anybody's life staring at a stick they just peed on.

Aside from pregnancy, there's HIV and a host of other STDs that could potentially damage your physical health to worry about. While some guys may not volunteer to put on a love glove, any dude who pressures you to have sex with him without wearing a condom is a selfish prick. Your body is your temple, and if he isn't willing to don his armor before entering your chambers, he shouldn't be granted permission. Besides, if he doesn't want to wear a condom with you, he most likely didn't strap one on with the last girl he slept with, and who knows where that skank's been.

A WORD ON
Cleanliness

While teenage boys might not understand that a woman's vagina is a warm, moist haven for bacteria, adult men should know better than to stick an unwashed grubby finger into your vajayjay. And in the case that you and your lover boy partake in anal play, he should NEVER double dip. Red flag if your man isn't conscious about contaminating your cooter.

Red-Flag Rule #24: If a guy doesn't even *reach* for a condom the first time you have sex, he doesn't respect you or your body.

WTF? *"I dated a guy who had herpes (and didn't tell me), who slept with me anyway and gave me herpes, and then said he did so knowingly so that I'd be stuck with him."*

Naturally, we understand that as your relationship with a guy becomes more serious—and presumably more committed—the two of you may decide to ditch the condoms, given you're on another method of birth control (and the pull-out method does not count; it's like playing Russian roulette with your ovaries!). If that's the case, your boyfriend should have no qualms getting tested for STDs, and we don't want to hear any whining about how bad the Q-tip test hurts.

BIG RED-FLAG STORY:

"A couple of guys I knew in college formed a 'Sans-Rubber Club.' They basically held a contest to see who could convince the most girls to sleep with them without wearing a condom."

Just FYI: Men who stray don't always use discretion—they often don't think twice about railing a porn star condomless, then turning around and sticking their dirty dicks in their unassuming girlfriends. Although many STDs can be taken care of rather painlessly when discovered in their early stages, if you let them sit and fester, a relatively easy-to-get-rid-of infection will wreak havoc on your reproductive organs. Cheating is one thing (and we'll talk about it in the next part), but giving you chlamydia because he slept with a stripper at Big Jim's Boobie Bungalow is quite another.

THE BOTTOM LINE:

Bedroom boundaries are necessary but not necessarily negative. Setting rules and discussing expectations allows you to relax and enjoy sex. Constantly fearing a weird or mean action from your man will make an orgasm less likely than discovering calorie-free beer. Trust should build as you and your lover gradually expand your sexual repertoire. When you go directly from kissing to kinky role-play, you don't establish the intimacy necessary to sustain a trusting relationship. Besides, without limits, you'd be doing everything with everyone and what's special (or even exciting) about that?

When you don't set boundaries or you continually allow your man to cross them, you open yourself up to exploitation. Empower yourself by knowing, asserting, and continuously reaffirming what you will and will not do to please your dude. Any guy who doesn't respect his girlfriend's rules for romping doesn't respect his girlfriend. He wants a sex slave, not a sweetheart.

TOP TEN RED FLAGS:
Details He Reveals about His Sexual Past

1. He doesn't *have* a sexual past.
2. He "accidentally" brought home a tranny one time.
3. He's participated in several swinger parties.
4. He had anal before vaginal sex.
5. He's been taking pole dancing lessons for the past year.
6. He's a serial streaker.
7. Clown noses turn him on.
8. His ex could give him five BJ's in one night. He expects the same from you.
9. He lost his virginity to a hooker.
10. He can't stand the smell of vagina.

WHETHER YOU'RE HAVING SEX with your boyfriend or jumping into bed with some dude on your second date, you should never feel like you have to do something you're just not comfortable with. If you clench up like a clamshell the moment your guy hints at sex, your body, more specifically your hoo-ha, is trying to tell you something.

Red-Flag Case Study #3

See how many red flags you can spot in just one story:

Super attracted to this guy I had gone out with a couple of times, we ended up making out on his couch one night, which led to the bedroom, which led to us being naked, which somehow led to the sixty-nine position.⚑ No seduction, no building of intimacy, no "Is this working for you?"⚑ —just an aggressive flip, and BAM! sixty-nine, genitals in my face.⚑ This was followed by an attempt to stick his finger up my rear (got to love that one).⚑ He then complained about having to wear a condom,⚑ and when he wasn't aroused enough to put it on, demanded for me to "fix this."⚑ As you can imagine, sex consisted of a series of aggressive thrusts with no thought of my pleasure.⚑ It was pretty obvious that I didn't have an orgasm, and he claimed I didn't enjoy having sex with him because he was wearing a condom.⚑

⚑ He's a wham-bam (probably no thank you) ma'am kinda guy. Going from making out to sixty-nine, in sixty-nine seconds, on a first hook-up? Not good.

🚩 He bypasses foreplay and is either bad in bed or selfish in bed. We'll put up with neither.

🚩 He's aggressive without asking, which shows he doesn't know how to communicate.

🚩 He should know better. Just as he should have asked before sticking his balls in her face, this guy should have made sure she was okay with that move before making it.

🚩 He doesn't make safe sex a priority.

🚩 He uses guilt to get her to abandon her principles.

🚩 He not only treats her like a slut, he also doesn't care about her pleasure. That attitude likely extends past the bedroom.

🚩 He puts the blame on her—and the condom—when in reality the problem is that he just sucks in bed.

Part Four

He Doesn't Love You

Chapter Twelve

He's Just Not Treating You Right

Perhaps you're in a steady relationship with a man and instead of treating you like the woman of his dreams (or even someone he enjoys spending time with), he's got you wondering if he even likes you at all. Maybe your boyfriend was so attentive that he wooed his way into your heart only to blindside you months, or even years, into the relationship by becoming an all-star asshole. Stay with a man long enough and his true colors will surface—even the smoothest of fellows can't keep up their suave facade forever.

Or perhaps you always kinda-sorta knew in the back of your mind that he wasn't behaving like a suitor should have, but proceeded anyway—for whatever reason, against all better judgment—and you're now in a full-blown relationship with a man who continues to take you for granted.

How you arrived at this juncture is irrelevant: Relationships have a way of running their courses, either uphill or downhill, and even the most committed, loving partnerships can hit a speed bump or dead end. When you've invested so much of yourself in a relationship, the desire for things to work out can be overwhelmingly strong, so much so that you have a hard time acknowledging seemingly obvious red flags, and an even harder time walking away from the offending man in question.

> *Red-Flag Rule #25:* If he's inconsiderate or insensitive during the so-called honeymoon phase, he's not going to suddenly start treating you better once the excitement and newness of the relationship wear off.

Two dates, two months, two years—it doesn't matter—the most important element of any relationship is how the man you're choosing to spend your time with treats you. He could be broke and busted, but treats you with the utmost respect and adoration (who cares if you're celebrating your one-year at Denny's while other customers gawk at your dude's manboobs?). Better that than he be successful, gorgeous, and rich but make you feel like shit.

A WORD ON
Why We Stay in Bad Relationships

Many of us have stayed in relationships with guys who just weren't treating us right. And we made excuses why we shouldn't just ditch these dicks. The following are common, yet completely unacceptable reasons to stay with a not-so-good dude:

- "I can't do any better."
- "No one else would want me."
- "I'm too old to get back out there."
- "Dating scares me."
- "My friends and family love him."
- "I'm totally dependent on him."
- "We used to be so good together."
- "I just want it to work out as it was supposed to."

- "I know he loves me deep down even if he doesn't show it."
- "I don't want to have to start over with another guy."

What you deserve, above all else, is to be treated right. And while "right" may mean different things to different women, here are some obvious signs that a man isn't honoring you the way you deserve. If the examples below sound all-too-familiar, put on those walking boots and hit the pavement.

He's inconsiderate.

Since we were kids, we've been told that actions speak louder than words. This is never truer than in how your man conducts himself toward you. Julie dated an athlete who had to wake up early for practice. When she would sleep at his place, he'd set his alarm for an hour before he needed to be up and then hit snooze at least fourteen times, waking her up in the process, when he knew she could have slept in. Not the biggest deal ever, but his only concern was clearly himself.

Here's another classic example: Let's say you're at a party, or even just having dinner at your place, and your guy gets up to refill his drink but he doesn't ask you if you need anything—his lack of attentiveness is definitely a red flag.

Sure, this particular gesture is small, but it's the little things that count. Any guy can do the obvious, like pick up a dozen roses on Valentine's Day; it's the small gestures that let you know he's thinking of you. And, while you shouldn't expect your guy to be on his best behavior at all times or be your servant (not that we'd mind that from time to time . . .), he should be thoughtful when the occasion calls for it.

BIG RED-FLAG STORY:

"The night of our engagement party, my ex-fiancé refused to pick me up because it was 'out of the way.' So I drove forty-five minutes out of the city to escort myself to what was supposed to be one of the greatest events of my life and walked in alone. Let me tell you, that was the beginning of the end."

Whether your guy doesn't call when he says he will, conveniently forgets your hang-out plans, or knowingly deprives you of sleep, he's too selfish to be dating anyone but himself. Give him a taste of his own medicine by going about your schedule for a week without considering him in it at all. He'll either realize how it feels to be left out of the equation and change his ways or he'll whine that you're not giving him enough attention without making the connection to his own behavior, a sign that he's both unintelligent and unable to be in a mature relationship. In the latter case, don't just leave him out for a week—extend the separation to forever.

He lies to you.

If, instead of sweet, sweet nothings, your guy consistently tells you sweet little lies, he may not trust that you can handle the truth. However, once you discover your guy is telling you tall tales, you most likely won't trust him as a result. A relationship without trust is like a building without a foundation—it'll stand for a little while, but as soon as a storm comes it'll inevitably fall apart.

The main explanation we hear as to why men lie is that they don't want to make us mad. Maybe your boyfriend's ex called him drunk one night and he tells you it was his sister because the chick means nothing to him and he'd rather not upset you. While he's trying to protect you, your guy clearly doesn't have enough faith in your ability to react rationally. And that's the red flag, not necessarily the lie itself. If your relationship is really a strong one, and you both love and trust each other, he shouldn't feel the need to withhold the truth.

Of course, some falsehoods really are harmless, or even for your own good: like if your guy tells you he was having lunch with his grandma when he was really picking up your engagement ring, or he offers to go around the corner to pick you up a coffee not to be nice but rather because he needs to relieve himself of some severe gastrointestinal issues and doesn't want to turn your bathroom into a biohazard. But these instances should be few and far between.

BIG RED-FLAG STORY:

"I've been dating my boyfriend for about eight months now. Our relationship has been very good, but, oddly, it's still a bit unstable: We see each other nearly every day but we haven't gotten into the 'I love you' phase yet. Recently, after one of our bigger, almost-breakup fights, I found out that he went to dinner with an old girlfriend from about two years back (he told me that he was having 'boys night' with his brother that night). I confronted him about it and he didn't deny it, and said that he didn't want to tell me because he didn't want me to worry. He confessed that they went to dinner, and then out for a drink, and that he was home by 11. I believed him. I get that people tell white lies from time to time but I'm not sure whether or not I should monitor this situation."

If you catch your man in a lie, or suspect that he's telling one, call him out on it and demand an explanation. A guy who rationalizes his decision to fib obviously doesn't really respect the idea that relationships are built on honest communication—and we think you should let him take his fabricating ways elsewhere.

He doesn't have your back.

You and your man should act as a team: He should stand up for you if his friend's being a dick and pick up the slack when you're having a bad day. You should do the same for him.

If your guy is constantly pointing out your flaws or correcting you (like when you say "uh huh" instead of "yes") in front of your friends, family, colleagues (or even total strangers), he's letting you, and the world, know that he really doesn't have your back. Not to say that your boyfriend should never disagree with you, but he definitely shouldn't pick you apart. Whether he belittles you in front of an audience or privately, you'll be left humiliated.

> **BIG RED-FLAG STORY:**
> "My boyfriend took me to a party, where I knew no one. Not only that, but one of the attendees happened to be his ex-girlfriend. When we got there, he didn't introduce me to anyone, not even his ex, making an awkward situation even more uncomfortable."

There is also the dude who not only doesn't have your back but will throw you under the bus to save his own hide—this guy isn't interested in being half of a united front, he's looking for a human shield to protect his obviously fragile ego.

WTF? *"My ex-boyfriend knew I was having multiple medical problems from a car accident, which led to overprescribed medication that seriously affected my well-being, but would tell people (behind my back) that he was pretty sure I was 'faking it.'"*

He doesn't show up.

Your boyfriend isn't some guy you're consistently hanging out with—he's your partner. As your right-hand man he should be both your teammate and cheerleader, and you his. So if guy starts bailing on, or forgetting about, important events—your law school graduation, your work promotion party, your comedy show—it's a sure sign that he doesn't consider your achievements, or you, to be all that important. And if you're not important to him, why would you date him? Find someone who'll be as dedicated to you as you are to him.

BIG RED-FLAG STORY:

"I was a theater major in college, and my sophomore year I landed a pretty big role in a major show. I really wanted the guy I was dating at the time to come, so I made sure to tell him about the performance way in advance. I told him in person, gave him a flier, and called him the day before to make sure he knew the time and place. He told me he would definitely be there.

"The day of the show, I texted him a couple of hours before the curtain went up, and he said he planned on coming. When I got out on stage, I scanned the audience to see if I could spot him. (Totally not supposed to do this, but hey, I was excited.) The house lights were still on, and the audience was less than one hundred people, so I should've been able to see him. He wasn't there. I figured I just couldn't find him and expected him to be waiting in the lobby with the rest of our friends after the show. He wasn't. Apparently, he'd 'forgotten' about my play that night."

He's not there for you during a crisis.

You never really know just how "there" your boyfriend is for you until shit hits the fan. Once it does, and you actually need him for something other than opening jars and reaching the top shelf of your closet, you'll quickly find out what kind of man he really is . . . or if he isn't one at all.

A dude who doesn't support you during a time of real need certainly won't hold your hand through the birth of your child, the deaths of your parents, and any other high-stress or grief-ridden situations that you're sure to face. Part of the perk of having a long-term beau is that you don't have to go through life's ups and downs alone. If he takes off when the going gets tough, you're better off going at it alone.

BIG RED-FLAG STORY:

"One night while watching God-knows-what reality TV show with my stoner boyfriend, whom I happened to be living with, I received a call from my mother letting me know my dad was in the hospital. He'd had a heart attack two years before, so I feared the worst and started crying hysterically. I rushed to get some clothes on, so we could get to the hospital ASAP.

"Instead of getting himself ready, however, my boyfriend just watched me. He said he didn't see why he needed to go too, even though I was in no condition to drive myself. After I convinced him to take me, he then wanted to know how long we were going to have to be at the hospital to see my dad, who may or may not have been dying."

He's grown indifferent toward you.

Red-Flag Rule #26: It's better to have loved and lost than to be stuck in a relationship that's no longer full of love at all.

Sure, after a couple of years of being with someone, you may not feel all giddy woo-hoo about him, but if the feelings of love between you seem to completely die and decompose, that's no good. If your guy really is the one for you, he'll show you that he wants to be with you ten, twenty, even fifty years down the road.

WTF? *"My ex-boyfriend's grand gesture to try to win me back—two years after we broke up—was a totally out-of-the-blue e-mail from him in which he said he wanted to try again and put in the effort to really make things works. There was one telltale sign, however, that he wasn't so set in his intentions: At the bottom of the e-mail I found 'Sent from my iPhone.' If he was so 'serious' about getting back together, how come he couldn't have used his phone to actually call me and tell me so?"*

Being comfortable with your partner is not the same as being indifferent to his or her presence. When your guy's attitude turns nonchalant, or even apathetic, your relationship with him is pretty much over. Writer and Nobel Peace Prize winner Elie Wiesel is credited with the often-quoted phrase that the opposite of love is not hate, it's indifference. And we have to agree with him.

In fact, divorced couples often pinpoint the beginning of the end of their marriages as the moment when they "checked out." A relationship hinges on your engagement in it—even fighting is better than completely not caring at all. If you feel like he's just going through the motions, it likely means there's a lack of emotion. A half-hearted boyfriend will only fill you with resentment. Find someone who'll love you without hesitation.

BIG RED-FLAG STORY:

"My roommate's boyfriend lives in Manhattan (we're in the Midwest) and she flies out every other weekend to visit him. When she comes back home, I ask her how her trip was, what they did, etc., and it's always the same story: They stayed at his place, he sat on the couch and watched football, drinking beer while she cooked meals for them. He's never once planned something fun for them to do together, not even going on a walk around Central Park or taking her out to dinner.

"She's told me that it bothers her how he just sits on his ass the whole weekend (while she waits on him), but she won't say anything because she's convinced she can't do any better. Of course, I'm not there on those visits, nor do I expect him to take her to a Broadway show every time she goes to the city, but, from my perspective, it's a huge red flag that they only get to spend six days a month together and he chooses to watch TV and get wasted."

He doesn't accept—or appreciate— you for who you are.

Typically, you fall in love with someone because you cherish their gifts and are willing to overlook their flaws. (Even better: You find some of these flaws endearing.)

You should never be made to feel inadequate for being you, especially by your dude. So you're not everything your man thinks you should be? Tough shit. If he wanted a dog he shouldn't be dating a cat. Never change who you are to please a man. Tell him he needs to love you as is or you're no longer willing to love him as is.

Red-Flag Rule #27: If your guy can't tolerate your quirks now, he's only going to resent them—and you—later.

BIG RED-FLAG STORY:

"Being an acupuncturist, I thought I wanted a boyfriend as equally spiritual as I was. When I began a relationship with a man who worked at one of those health retreats/boot camps where people pay an exorbitant amount of money to be told what to eat, when to sleep, and how long to exercise for an entire week, I was excited to be with someone who would understand me.

"After a couple of weeks, he felt the need to control what I ate, how much coffee I drank, etc. We started spending endless hours talking about how we could improve ourselves and continue to grow as individuals. The only problem was that every one of these 'discussions,' as he called them, soon became all about my supposed downfalls (most of which centered around me having emotions, a bad habit he thought should stop). When I told him that it really wasn't all that fun to always talk about the things he thought were wrong with me, he didn't understand what the problem was.

"I knew I had to get out of the relationship when I started hiding my Jack in the Box wrappers from him, since he'd berated me the first time he witnessed me give in to a fast-food craving."

He doesn't make you feel special.

Okay, so we're gonna get a little touchy-feely on you here. (Sorry.) Here goes: Your boyfriend is supposed to love you. He's supposed to make you feel like the most beautiful, intelligent, wonderful woman in the world. If he's not making you feel special, it's time to re-evaluate how he is making you feel. We'd take a wild guess it's something other than good.

WTF? *"On every gift-giving occasion, my ex-boyfriend would give me nothing and say 'It's the thought that counts.' What thought, you idiot? You didn't get me anything."*

Your boyfriend should be a positive presence in your life, treating you not just okay, well, or "good enough," but actually better than anyone else he knows. Therefore, a guy with a lot of female friends—let's define "a lot" as having more lady pals than male ones—who tend to literally hang on him, as well as on his every word, raises a big red flag.

This isn't about jealousy—it's about respect: If you notice that your boyfriend puts other women before you, don't try to excuse his behavior by convincing yourself that he and these ladies are just really close and have known each other for a long time. When a guy has a serious girlfriend, this is not a valid excuse.

> *Red-Flag Rule #28:* If the guy you're dating is friends with all the girls he used to sleep with—and also expects to be friends with you, should you break up—he's delusional.

Meagan dated this guy who was super attentive and just all-around great . . . she thought. When she lost the key to her car, he drove her to get her spare—and even bought her a special key-hider to attach to her car. But she soon realized that his seemingly chivalrous behavior extended to his bevy of female friends, and he'd run to their rescue the moment they'd call on him to help them move, fix their computers—you name it—even when he and Meagan had plans.

If a guy is going to be at a girl's beck and call, it should be his girlfriend's, and hers alone. As one of our blog readers advised in a comment: "If you're dating someone who always puts another girl's needs before yours . . . dump him and run." We couldn't agree more.

BIG RED-FLAG STORY:

"Starting with our very first date, my ex would talk about his most recent ex. I learned about this girl's favorite kind of Chapstick, fake blonde hair, the time she peed in her pants, oh, and the time they had sex upstairs at her parents' house during a shiva call. He knew it bothered me, yet he continued bringing up his past relationships. I knew about three girls from this guy's past, all of whom he'd been in love with (stalked) in college. (He listed them all for me one time when we were stuck in traffic.) Any time I talked about a friend's relationship, he'd bring up yet another failed love story of his. Soon enough, it seemed like he pretty much fell for any girl and immediately jumped from attraction to love. When he told me he loved me, it came out of nowhere—after an hour-long bitch session about how his ex screwed him over."

THE BOTTOM LINE:

Whether your boyfriend just doesn't treat you right once in a while or all the time, his behavior needs to be evaluated and corrected—now—or you need to tell him to find an unspecial girl to match his unspecial treatment because you're too precious to be passed over like that.

If your friends sit you down and tell you you've changed for the worse since dating a new guy, don't get defensive—believe them. Often the people close to you serve as good barometers for gauging whether or not your guy is treating you right. If your most trusted comrades work up the nerve to voice their dissatisfaction, definitely listen up. While they aren't privy to private moments when your man actually shows you just how much he adores and respects you, it speaks volumes if the only time he's nice to you is behind closed doors, and it's time to stop making excuses for his behavior and face reality. (Besides, is he really being all that nice? Even a saltine cracker tastes like a fresh-baked baguette when you're starving.)

The people closest to you have seen you at your best, your worst, and every shade in between. They know when you're happiest, and they can tell when you're not doing so great. When they notice a difference in you that seems to coincide with the start of your relationship, you can't really blame them for speaking up.

Your friends' and family's thoughts usually reflect what your gut is already telling you: You know when you're not being treated right by your boyfriend. You'll not only feel put down and pushed aside, but that uneasy feeling in the pit of your stomach is your intuition telling you that you deserve better.

> *Red-Flag Rule #29:* If you have to think twice about whether or not your man is treating you right, you're already thinking too hard.

TOP TEN RED FLAGS:
How He Treats the Waitress

1. He nicknames her "sugar tits."
2. He demands she select his entree.
3. He attempts to speak Spanish by adding "o" to every word.
4. He won't look her in the eye.
5. He speaks condescendingly, as if she's a learning-disabled seven year old.
6. He has questions about everything on the menu, from sauces to bread thickness to whether they use sea, kosher, or table salt.

7. He sends his food back several times.

8. He makes ridiculous requests, like "Please don't cook my meal with any oils, pepper, or heat."

9. He asks for ketchup and when she doesn't bring it in 30 seconds, he goes into the kitchen to get it himself.

10. He threatens to get her fired when she messes up a minor detail of the order.

He's Never Going to Propose

Some gals look forward to their wedding days starting in kindergarten. They just can't wait to don the white dress and walk down the aisle toward a man with the looks of Brad Pitt, charm of George Clooney, and faithfulness of Matt Damon.

While this may or may not be you, many of us have at least thought about being a bride someday. Most people expect to one day solidify a committed relationship by getting married. While this may not be the goal for every couple, marriage is our society's way of officially labeling a long-term partnership, so it's worth addressing.

Red-Flag Rule #30: If your boyfriend only talks about marrying you when he's drunk, you probably shouldn't start planning your bridal registry.

Even though we've come a long way, we still have to sit around and wait for our damn rings since men still typically propose marriage. While you and your guy will decide together when it's time to take your relationship to the next level, he gets solo initiative to actually enact this major step by, traditionally, popping that big question and presenting you with a schmancy ring. If you're the type who likes to be in control, this can be a bit nerve-wracking . . . especially as your friends and acquaintances start going to the chapel before you.

Marital Intentions

You may confuse wanting to get married with actually knowing that it's the right decision for you and your boyfriend. Since marriage is presumably for life, nothing bad ever came from waiting just a bit longer to be sure. On the other hand, moving too fast has a relatively poor track record of producing happy long-lasting marriages. Don't take this decision lightly. "Everyone else is doing it" is not a legit reason to get hitched. And if you're thinking your guy should propose after you've been official for a few months or weeks, you need your head examined.

If you've never broached the subject of marriage further than drunkenly serenading your dude while out at a club with Beyoncé's "Single Ladies," as Natasha tends to do when she's had one too many shots of Patrón, you may be signaling to him that you're not actually serious about him wanting to "put a ring on it" either. Or, if you've been dating exclusively for years without a real discussion about your future together—even if to simply conclude that you're not ready to even think about it seriously yet—chances are your guy isn't plotting to get down on one knee.

He tells you he's not interested in getting married.
Doesn't get more obvious than this, ladies. Some men don't believe in the institution of marriage. Maybe they don't like the idea of being locked in, their parents' divorce left a serious impact, or they

have an ideological reason why holy matrimony sounds like total baloney. If your guy clearly states he doesn't want to get married, to you or to anyone, you're most likely not going to change his mind—no matter how much cooler, cuter, and come-hither-er you are than his past girlfriends.

> *Red-Flag Rule #31:* If you find out your guy has never said "I love you," even though he previously dated another girl seriously for years, this information could signal intimacy issues.

When one person in the relationship wants to get married (presumably you) and the other doesn't, you have a fundamental difference on your hands that needs to be addressed. We don't advise giving your boyfriend a deadline-oriented ultimatum (as in "We need to be married by x date or I'm leaving you") or being one of those lame girls who drop not just hints, but marry-me bombs (like circling rings in the Tiffany's catalogue and "accidentally" planting it in your man's briefcase).

However, if marriage is what you're after, and it's not even on your man's radar, your relationship will be unfulfilling for both you and your noncommittal man. You shouldn't stay in a relationship in which each person wants—and expects—different things.

BIG RED-FLAG STORY:

"One of my guy friends is single, approaching thirty, and has no intention of getting married. He's an active online dater and he tells women from the get-go that he's not going to settle down—maybe ever. However, many of these ladies see his up-fronted-ness as a challenge to see if they can tame a him . . . like being able to change his bachelor status is some kind of game or accomplishment. Unfortunately for them, he not only doesn't have any interest in marriage, but he also has no clue what he wants in a woman. After going on probably about fifty dates, no one can even meet his expectations enough for him to want to be in a relationship for any longer than two weeks."

He uses marriage as a bargaining chip.

The context in which your guy brings up marriage is very important. If your dude only talks of tying the knot to guilt you into staying with him, to get something from you, or to stay out of the doghouse, don't fall for his false promises of imminent matrimony. Clearly, he doesn't get the point: Getting hitched won't fix a bad relationship, it just makes getting out of one more difficult.

A guy who's willing to use marriage to mess with your head probably shouldn't be trusted with your heart. Get a man who values honesty enough to be truthful with you regarding where your relationship is going. Don't stand for a guy who dangles the marriage carrot but doesn't intend to present you with at least one carat.

BIG RED-FLAG STORY:

"I had just moved across the country for grad school when, three days later, my boyfriend came to visit. Well, he wasn't there specifically to see me, he adamantly insisted, but rather to attend an event with his pseudo-celebrity friend. After this event, he ended up in his friend's hotel room with some girls and, as I found out later, made out with one of them.

"When he told me this information, I told him things were over between us, horrified that the second I moved away, he not only cheated on me, but did so right down the street from my new place. That's when he started crying and said, 'But I wanted to marry you,' using this loose promise of a future together as a way to make me stay. Against my better judgment, I did. For two more years. He never proposed."

He keeps you a secret.

After a couple of months or so of dating, a guy will more likely than not introduce you to his family and friends. After a couple of years, his doing so is a given. In fact, by that point in your relationship you should be close enough with his crew to know pertinent details of his pals' lives and have spent quality time with them. (Of course, a guy who isn't close with his family or has no friends is a different story and could signal red flags in itself.)

If your man doesn't tell his parents, or anyone close to him, about you, he's clearly not seeing your relationship as one that will culminate with you walking down a rose-petal-strewn aisle. So if a wedding is what you're looking for, you may want to look elsewhere for a guy who's glad to call you his girl.

BIG RED-FLAG STORY:
"Perhaps I should have been more concerned when I learned that my thirty-five-year-old boyfriend hadn't told his folks that we were living together. It would have been one thing if he didn't communicate with his parents all that much, but given how close they were, it was pretty abnormal for him to conceal information from them, especially when said information was pertinent to who he was and how he was living his life."

He's not willing to put you first.

If a man is truly committed to you, and your relationship is on the road to marriage, he will make you an integral part of his daily life.

And if he's not, well, he'll also make that perfectly plain by putting everything from work to working out ahead of you.

> *Red-Flag Rule #32:* If a guy tells you "I wish we'd met each other later in life" . . . he means he still wants time to sow his wild oats, not settle down.

For example, a beau who consistently makes plans with his boys on Fridays and Saturdays, the universal date nights, without asking about your plans, is not that serious about a real commitment. While he shouldn't have to "check in" with you constantly like a castrated nancy-boy, he should make time for you, if he's truly committed to being with you. This guy clearly still relishes his single life, but unfortunately for him, he's got you, his girlfriend. He can't have both.

If long-term commitment is what you want, ask him to put you first. When he isn't willing to do that, the relationship won't last. You should be a featured character in your guy's life story, not an extra walking through the background.

BIG RED-FLAG STORY:

"Marijuana was far more important to my ex than I was. More than a few times he turned down sex to go smoke pot with his roommate. He'd often show up to hang out with me so stoned that we couldn't hold a real conversation. If I'd given him an ultimatum of me or the pot, I am one hundred percent positive he'd have chosen the weed."

Aside from showing you that he puts you first by including you in his schedule, your guy should actually vocalize this, not leave his feelings for you up to your interpretation. This means affirming that he indeed loves you and is committed to your relationship. He should be willing to have, and even initiate, open conversations with you about where your relationship is headed.

He makes plans for his future . . . and they don't include you.

Red-Flag Rule #33: If your man's got marriage—to you—on the brain, he'll eventually start speaking in we's. If he says "when I get married" rather than "when we get married," he's not thinking about anything long term . . . with you, anyway.

If you're in a serious relationship, you and your man are presumably thinking about, even just theoretically, your future together. When your boyfriend talks about the next ten or twenty years of his life and you're M-I-A, he's probably not thinking about making you his M-R-S.

Also notice how flexible—or inflexible—he is about accommodating your life plan. If he's unwilling to move to another city or state to be closer to your family, or to allow you to take your dream job, he's showing you that he's unwilling to modify his plans so that you can be part of them. When a future together is not in the cards, forget about the past you share and stop dating the guy.

BIG RED-FLAG STORY:

"After dating long distance for nine months, my boyfriend convinced me to move from my hometown in the Midwest out to California on the premise that he would propose to me soon after. Well, when I got out there, and we began living together, not only did he spend my birthday golfing with his boys, but I soon found out from his buddy's girlfriend that he had made arrangements to move to Scottsdale. Since I had no idea that this was his plan, I didn't know how to answer her when she asked if I was looking forward to moving to a new city after I had just relocated two months prior. Obviously, he wasn't planning on asking me to go with him."

WTF? *"One night after moving in with my boyfriend, thinking we were on our way to holy matrimony, I received a call from him while he was out of town on business. However he didn't actually call me, his cell phone had dialed me from his pocket, and I could hear him talking with his colleagues. In the conversation he told them that he was questioning his decision to move in together and (I quote) thought he could do better."*

He treats you like you're his backup plan.

We hate to say it, but some men enter into relationships simply to kill time. They're looking for consistent sex, someone to hang out with, someone to take care of them, someone to take care of—until, that is, someone better comes along.

Sometimes the guy has another girl in mind . . . she's just not available yet. You'll probably notice the more common signs that he's not going to propose, like not introducing you to his family or not making plans for vacations together more than a few months in advance. However, his noncommittal behavior will be coupled with the presence of a close female friend or references to "the one who got away."

BIG RED-FLAG STORY:

"I was dating a guy and things were going so well that we moved in together after just three months. Turned out, he was still in love (and actively trying to back together) with his long-time on-again, off-again girlfriend, whose child (not his) apparently called him 'Daddy.' I later found out that while we were sharing a home together, he was busy making her a massive scrapbook as a means to try to win her back. He was compelled to make said scrapbook after his ex called him up to inform him that she was getting serious with another guy. Instead of giving a recip-rocally respectful response about how he too has moved on and is very, very happy living with someone new (me), he went and made her a fucking scrapbook."

A man who doesn't really want to be with you in the long run is not worth wasting time with in the present. This guy doesn't love you, he loves that you'll love him while he waits for the girl he actually wants. We suggest you don't play second fiddle in the orchestrated love life in this guy's head.

THE BOTTOM LINE:
If you're anticipating a white wedding and your man is only look-ing as far into the future as Sunday's football game, you're likely operating on different life clocks. He may fear commitment, but his apprehension could also be because he knows that you're not the one. Too many women sit around and wait for their man's cold feet to get warmer when in reality his feet aren't the problem, his heart is.

Or maybe his head's the issue here: While women generally see marriage as a finish line, many men see it as a starting line . . . for a race they don't really want to run. You can train and encourage him, but he's the one who must ultimately decide to compete.

While the romantic notion of a soul mate is appealing, a ton of factors come into play when determining the trajectory of any given relationship. Being compatible as a couple is not just about having similar likes and values; it's about wanting the same things out of life, as well as wanting these things to happen on roughly the same schedule. (Timing is certainly everything when it comes to coupling—how often have we thought "if only we'd met at another time . . ." in regard to some guy from the past?)

When you start to get the feeling that the only question your man's gonna pop for now is what you're cooking for dinner, decide whether you can wait or whether you should find another guy altogether. If the flags in this chapter sounded familiar, we suggest the latter option.

WTF? *"I know a guy who gives girls empty Tiffany's ring boxes when he breaks up with them."*

TOP TEN RED FLAGS:
What He Gets You for Valentine's Day

1. A lip hair bleach kit
2. A framed picture of himself
3. A Happy Meal toy
4. A homemade positive affirmation CD titled "Your Man, Your Master"
5. A thong with "I'd rather be taking it up the ass" written on the front
6. An expensive bottle of wine . . . that your parents gave him for his birthday two years ago
7. A gift card to his favorite restaurant
8. A scale
9. A tattoo of you riding a comet on his back
10. A six-pack of Natty Light

Chapter Fourteen

He's Using You

Being the kind, caring women that we are, giving is our second nature. Doing nice things for the people we love literally makes us feel good. Studies both in female animals and in humans show that women release that oxytocin hormone we mentioned in Chapter 2 not just during intimate moments but also when we perform maternal caretaking duties. And since giving and giving some more makes us feel all warm and fuzzy inside, we often have a difficult time recognizing when we're being taken advantage of . . . by, let's say, our boyfriends.

Men who habitually use women—whether for emotional, sexual, social, or financial gain—are virtuosos at playing our heartstrings. Users are master con artists who know exactly what to say and how to act in order to get what they want. Once they've wormed and wiggled their way into our lives with future promises and empty flattery, these charlatans set up shop, exploiting our resources for their personal gain.

We're not saying that each person's contribution to a given relationship is always going to be perfectly equal—that's why you hear all those references to give and take. What we are saying is that there are guys out there, wolves in sheep's clothing, if you will, who have built a life preying on the love of a good woman.

When you hear of a man's using a woman, your first thought might be that he just wants to get laid. Since we already covered a guy who treats you like a slut in Chapter 2, the flags below are the less obvious, but equally noxious, ways a dude may suck you dry.

He treats you like a trophy wife.

While it's great to feel like your man's top dog, he shouldn't strut you around like a pedigree at Westminster so his ego can take a victory lap. Whether he uses you to up his status on the coolness hierarchy or to make himself feel more like a man, a dude who wants to be with you for your hotness, and how desirable you make him look by association, reduces you to your physical assets, which is downright demeaning and devalues all the other wonderful qualities you have to offer.

A boyfriend who really loves you is going to be excited to bring you around his peeps, so they can see for themselves just how fabulous you truly are. But there's a big difference between showing you off and using you to impress his buddies or coworkers (or, worse, to make his ex-girlfriend jealous). Watch out if he parades you around a room of bigwigs without allowing you to have a real conversation with anyone—he's treating you like a possession bought to impress and not a person to be cherished.

Guys who treat women like trophies are pretty much misogynists. Typically they simply expect you to be seen, not heard, likening you to a bit of bling to make them shine brighter. Should you have some sparkle of your own, aside from your appearance, of course, they won't be having it—your true awesomeness will be too much of a distraction from themselves.

BIG RED-FLAG STORY:

"While out to dinner with this guy I made a joke. When he didn't even smile I said, jokingly, 'Hey that was funny. Did you know I was that funny?' He replied, 'Well, I guess you just don't show that side of yourself to me.' We went to dinner a second time, and I again said something that was indeed funny. To which he responded, 'Look, your job is to sit there and look pretty.'"

Before your man brainwashes you into thinking you're little more than arm candy, evaluate exactly what it is about you that he loves. If every aspect you come up with is skin deep, forget your depthless dude and find a guy who wants to show off all of you, including that which doesn't simply meet the eye.

He treats you like his housewife.

There are guys who can't take care of themselves, and then there are men who are completely capable but would rather have a woman handle their domestic duties.

This latter type of dude typically moves the relationship along at exponential speed. Believing it when he says you're the perfect woman for him, you go along for the ride and before you know it, you're practically living at his house and have taken over all the traditional wifely chores. One night you're dating, the next morning you're pressing his shirts. One month he's wining and dining you, the next you're slaving over a hot stove.

> *Red-Flag Rule #34:* If some dude tells you on a first date that you'll make a great mom to his kids, he's not looking for a partner to share the rest of his life with, he's looking for a babysitter.

If you didn't sign up to be your guy's wifey, yet you're constantly playing his maid, chef, and nanny—and you aren't really sure what's in this arrangement for you—we hate to say it, but you're being used.

BIG RED-FLAG STORY:
"I had a friend who 'dated' four different women at the same time. One to sleep with, one to cook for him, one to take out on dates, and one to show his parents."

He covets your connections.

You happen to live a fabulous life: You've got an enviable list of industry contacts, attend all the best parties, and have a job most of your friends would forfeit a few fingers for. You've grown accustomed to everyone, from your best friend's little sister to your aunt's new beau, wanting you to help them or hook them up. When you're as well connected as you are, scavengers come with the territory. It's not what you know, but who you know—or maybe even who you are—that has everyone so interested in getting a piece.

When you're connected, chances are you're going to come across a few fellas who'd rather sleep their way to the top than put in the leg work to make it happen for themselves. Pay attention to a man's questions and how he acts around your powerful pals. When you feel like you're a shortcut, tell the guy he doesn't make the boyfriend cut because he's lazy and insincere, two characteristics the man of your dreams shouldn't possess.

BIG RED-FLAG STORY:
"A blast from the past I hadn't seen or talked to in five years contacted me via Facebook. He was still a writer and living in

New York City, and when he found out I worked in Hollywood, it sounded like such a glamorous life to him. So glamorous that he told me he had a crush on me and wanted to get to know me better. I fell for it. (I later realized that he only contacted me whenever my movie-star employer did something that made the news.)

"When he visited me in L.A., the first thing he said was 'Tell me about your career.' Not 'How have you been? How's life? How was your day?' Just, 'Tell me about your career.' Then he asked me if I went to any Grammy parties. From there the date just went downhill: He was rude and inconsiderate, pretending he was interested in me, while he sneaked in questions about who I knew and my contacts in the entertainment industry. Haven't spoken to him since."

He's always at your place.

We get it. Your boyfriend lives in a three-bedroom shithole with four other dudes, has plastic lawn chairs for furniture and empty kegs for end tables, and the only sources of entertainment are the rumpled *Playboy* magazines on the floor of every room.

When frat boys have a better setup than your man, of course you're going to choose to hang at your place rather than subject yourself to his sticky floors and the smell of sheets desperately in need of changing. But if your guy's always over, helping himself to your hard-earned luxuries, and starts inviting his homeboys to kick it on your three-piece sectional, he's taking the phrase *"mi casa es su casa"* just a little too far. You might want to find out if it's you or your stuff he likes more before he asks to full-on move in. If the guy makes a habit of coming over when all the big fights are on—and you're not even a sports fan—check your cable bill, sister. He's using you.

BIG RED-FLAG STORY:

"After dating for a month, this guy asked me to move in. My first thoughts were that he must want something (other than sex, which we'd already had plenty of), but I moved in anyway. The next month he tried to evict me. Come to find out, he had told his friends that he only invited me to move in with him because he wanted my things. Once evicted, I had thirty days to get all of my stuff out of his house or he would be able to keep everything. When that happened, and he refused to give me back my very expensive belongings, we went to court."

Maybe your guy isn't just always at your place, but after months of dating he has yet to invite you to see his man cave. Yes, he could be embarrassed about his impoverished living conditions, he might still live with his parents . . . or he may not have any place to invite you! You might want to look into it. Think about what time he tends to stop by and the reasons he gives for wanting to see you. If he always swings by late and comes even when you tell him you're busy, your guy could be using you for a warm bed to rest his head. Set some boundaries and if he can't honor them, tell him he's out of the game.

WTF? *"I met a guy at a friend of a friend's party and, after some light flirting turned into a heavy make-out session, we ended up back at my place. I noticed that the guy smelled a little weird, but figured it was nothing. For the next three weeks we kept ending up at my place—he always wanted to sleep over. This was fine, since we really hit it off, but I got a little suspicious as to why we never went to his place. Turned out he was homeless. Not bum-on-the-street homeless, but literally-didn't-have-a-home-and-usually-slept-in-a-youth-hostel homeless."*

He never picks up the tab.

Three months of dating, and somewhere along the way you went from going Dutch to keeping your man fed. Whether he happens to always "forget his wallet," is "waiting to get paid," or mysteriously disappears every time the check arrives, if your guy's always coming up with excuses for why he can't foot the bill for your dates, or never fulfills those I'll-get-the-next-one promises, he may be taking advantage of you for the nice dinners and free booze you provide him.

Some men will try to get away with paying for nothing based on the argument that they're only accompanying you because you wanted to go out and, if given the choice, they would not be spending their money doing the sort of things the two of you have been doing. To these parasitic dudes, we say: good luck finding a girl who wants to sit at home on Friday nights watching you play video games and eat Taco Bell. You cheap motherfuckers.

While extenuating circumstances may prevent you and your man from contributing equally to the relationship, you should think about whether or not he's worth the wallet drain.

BIG RED-FLAG STORY:
"My ex believed that people in a relationship were supposed to share their money. Of course, my money was for spending on dates, while his so-called 'hard-earned money' (he spent most of his time at work sleeping) was for saving. By the time we broke up I was short quite a sum."

You're fully supporting him.

You want to be his soul provider (Michael Bolton shout-out number two!) but instead you're his sole provider. While there's nothing wrong with helping a guy out from time to time, your man should treat you like his sexy momma, not his Daddy Warbucks. If the latter is the case, we guarantee the sun will not come out tomorrow, or any day thereafter.

A user creates an unbalanced relationship that's bound to leave you crippled, both financially and emotionally. If you continue to fund his foibles, you'll end up resenting him for breaking your bank account and resenting yourself for giving him a key to your safe.

And, ladies, please watch out for the I-just-moved-across-the-country-to-be-with-you guy who acts like you owe him for his "sacrifice" and expects you to make it up to him by paying his way. One of our blog reader's ex-boyfriends did just that and, instead of trying to line up a source of income before making the move (as she suggested), he went with the "it'll work out when I get there" plan and spent six months living on her dime, while spending all his savings on magazines and video games, which he entertained himself with between half-assed attempts to find employment. In the end, the dude wound up working part-time stocking shelves at Wal-Mart and dropping lines to his girlfriend like "Oh, you'll just be the breadwinner and I'll be a house-husband." Don't fall for these tricks: Send your mooching man packing so he can go back to where he came from.

BIG RED-FLAG STORY:

"I dated a guy who was a struggling actor in Los Angeles, meaning he had little to no money. For the most part, I paid for us when we went to dinners or movies, since I had a pretty good job. One month when he was really low on cash, I offered to help him out with his rent and told him he could just pay me when he got the money. Well, one month of 'help' turned into him asking me to pay his entire rent the next month. I really liked the guy, and he seemed crazy about me—constantly telling me how much he loved me—so I paid it.

"Then, one day he asked me to check his e-mail while I was at work (he was trying to get to an audition and forgot the address). That's when I noticed a folder titled 'Karen' (the name of his ex-girlfriend). Although I know you're not supposed to snoop, I opened the folder anyway and read through some of their e-mails. Come to find out, not only did she pay his rent while they were together, but he'd recently asked her for money—and she'd given him $250. So, basically, we were both supporting his broke ass. And, no, he never did pay me back."

THE BOTTOM LINE:
A man who loves you will appreciate your giving ways but never take advantage of them. A user, on the other hand, doesn't value you; he values whatever you have that will get him ahead. So, before you go give all your assets away, make sure you know what your babe brings to the table in return. The two of you should be living symbiotically, each contributing to, and benefiting from, the relationship. If your dude's a parasite and you're his host, he'll thrive while you'll struggle to remember how this one-sided arrangement happened.

The second you stop handing out your connections, let your looks fade, or refuse to pay his rent, he'll detach and find another host to leech off of. And good riddance: Without your exploiting ex you'll be able to regenerate not just your bank account but also your self-worth.

TOP TEN RED FLAGS:
Signs He's Just Too Broke

1. His bedroom is someone else's living room.
2. He goes to temple on Saturday mornings just to get the free Bar Mitzvah smorgasbord.
3. He goes through your recycling every time he comes over.
4. He has several unfinished tattoos.
5. He spends six of his last eight dollars on a Carl's Jr. Bacon Cheeseburger.
6. His desk, chair, bed, and couch are fashioned from stacked milk crates.
7. He buys condoms at the 99-cent store.
8. You gave him an iPhone for Christmas. He gave you an IOU.
9. He pounds beers in the parking lot before you go into a bar.
10. He takes you out for a nice dinner . . . at 7-11.

Chapter Fifteen

He's Cheating on You

Finding out your beau has betrayed you by bed-hopping hurts like a kick to your baby maker. Not only have you been let down by the person you've trusted with your heart, you've been lied to, humiliated, and forsaken for another woman.

A man who cheats has given himself permission to do so. Whether he thinks monogamy simply isn't innate to men or feels that you're not fulfilling your duties as his girlfriend, a cheater always finds a way to justify his unfaithful behavior, if not to you then to himself. After all, he's the one who matters most.

WTF? *"I just recently began posting pictures for family and friends on Facebook. Lo and behold, my ex tried to friend me. We had dated for a year, lived together for six months, and then I caught him having sex with one of his coworkers on our sofa. Needless to say, it was over—I threw him out. He broke back into our apartment, trashed the place, and tried to set the sofa on fire (hooray for flame retardant fabric!). I had to get a restraining order against him, and now he wants back into my life via Facebook? I don't think so."*

Any way you twist it, cheating is by far the most selfish thing a man can do. Not only does he cause you incredible emotional pain and destroy the trust upon which your relationship is built, he's also risking your ability to trust another man. Ever. Again. Most girls who've been cheated on instinctively grow a hard shell that future men won't be able to penetrate.

And while we're on the topic of penetration, it's important to note that a man need not put his poker in another gal's fire to cheat on you. Even though we typically think of cheating as sexual infidelity, a man can cheat emotionally by flirting, spending time with, or fantasizing about another chick. In fact, a purely emotional affair can be at least as heart-rending as discovering your man's been doing it with some skank he just met. If your man gets drunk at a bar and hooks up with a random girl, it's far less an offense (though still very hurtful) than that of the guy who develops an intense emotional bond with another woman. The latter dude builds intimacy with this mistress—sharing things with her that should be reserved for you.

WTF? *"After moving into my boyfriend's studio apartment, there were a few seemingly petty incidents in which I stormed out (because I couldn't go into another room) and he would say 'don't bother coming home.' As it turned out, he would initiate fights just so that I would storm out and he could use the apartment to sleep with other women."*

Finding out another woman is occupying our man's attention, time, or bed definitely gives a one-two punch to our self-esteem. Some women have a no-tolerance policy about cheating—if their men stray, they're out the door. Others, however, might choose to stay with their boyfriends after being betrayed, hoping to rebuild the trust and intimacy that was essentially destroyed. Should you find out your man is messing around, know that your relationship with him is forever changed. There's no such thing as a clean slate. So instead of trying to "start over," you and your wandering-eyed Willy need to realistically assess the damage and design a plan for proceeding that works for both parties.

Habitual cheaters may be adept at throwing off a woman's scent, but a gal's intuition is a powerful tool. (One unexplained late night or a defensive response and every cell in your body will know.) But if you're not too instinctive, we've compiled the flags below to help you recognize a man on the make.

He's always defensive.

If you ask your man how his day was and he says something like, "Great! I mean, okay. I was alone all day. Doing nothing . . . with no one. Why?," we'd put money on the fact that he's sleeping around (or at least wants to).

Cheaters often become paranoid, imagining suspicion in everything you say and do, even when your words and actions are unrelated to questioning his honesty. When he interprets every question you ask him as an interrogation, he's probably hiding something. As his paranoia increases, so does the likelihood that he's cheating.

BIG RED-FLAG STORY:
"My boyfriend of two years suddenly started hiding his cell phone from me. When I'd ask who he was texting, he'd get pissy and say, 'A friend! God!' I later flat-out confronted him about cheating and he said I was the one who was totally crazy and paranoid. I eventually looked through his phone and confirmed he was two-timing me."

He accuses *you* of cheating.

We're not precisely sure what psychology lies behind this crackpot move, but loads of women have reported the phenomenon. Our guess is that this guy is projecting his guilt onto you, hoping you'll admit some form of blame so that he doesn't feel like the only villain in the relationship. Or maybe he truly believes you're unfaithful because he assumes that, like himself, everyone else also lies and cheats.

This devious dude may get super possessive, needing to know where you are and whom you're with at all times. His sudden vigilance is probably due to one of the following: (1) If he knows where you are, he knows where not to go with his second sweetheart; (2) he wants you to think he's so obsessed with you that he couldn't possibly cheat; or (3) he's looking for evidence to frame you as the transgressor. Don't be tricked into taking the fall for his philandering fiascoes.

BIG RED-FLAG STORY:

"All of a sudden my guy started asking me questions about my Facebook page—saying I needed to explain why 'all these guys' (totally just friends) were writing on my wall, etc. He later confessed he was using my password to break into my Facebook and my Gmail and started grilling me about messages I'd gotten from my male cousin and one of my professors, which were of course totally harmless. (A word to the wise: Never share passwords with your significant other.) I later found out that around this time he had randomly run into his ex at a bar and went home with her. Nothing really happened—they slept in the same bed—but he felt guilty and was looking for anything suspicious that I'd done so he could justify his actions."

Sharing Passwords

Nothing good ever comes from swapping passwords with your guy. Even if your relationship is healthy, you will be tempted to check his e-mail and Facebook messages, and trust us, no matter what you find, you won't like it. Any shady messages from women will only confirm he's cheating on you (which you likely suspected anyway), and any that are innocent will only be misinterpreted and/or blown out of proportion, leaving you hurt and your guy feeling like you don't trust him. So not worth it.

He's shady with his phone (Part II).

Just like the player from Chapter 3, a cheater may have deviant phone habits: snatching up his cell the second it rings, responding to midnight texts from his "brother," taking his calls in another room, or continually erasing his call log and text history. While the behavior is similar, the situation with a cheater is completely different—you're not just hooking up with this guy, you're in a committed relationship with him. The stakes are higher and your hurt will be deeper when you find out he's double-dipping his dipstick.

BIG RED-FLAG STORY:

"I had been seriously dating this guy for over a year. We were exclusive, but he did have a close female friend that I was never allowed to meet. He wouldn't take her phone calls when I was in the room: He would call her back from another room or after I'd left his place. When they were hanging out together, he wouldn't answer calls from me. Then he took a long weekend, driving over four hours to be at her graduation. He made it clear that he did not want my company."

Don't hesitate to question this Lothario the next time he tries to convince you that the "I Wanna Sex You Up" ringtone is not his other lover. Confront your man outright—he'll likely crack under pressure (they tend to do that).

He leaves a trail of evidence.

The thong—and hooker boots—you found in your guy's apartment weren't left there by his mother. The perfume you smelled on his shirt isn't his new laundry detergent. No one gets sexted by "accident." If the evidence starts to stack up against your guy, don't deny the case: Your cheating beau may be stupid enough to leave clues for you to find, but when caught he'll no doubt attempt to put together a charming defense that you'll so much want to believe. Recognize he's guilty and find a dude whose only crime is loving you too much.

BIG RED-FLAG STORY:
"I was dating a guy for six months and every time I returned from a trip, I'd find a random piece of jewelry in his bed. I believed him the first couple of times when he said the items belonged to his platonic female friends. (Supposedly, he would have parties when I was out of town and all of his friends would wind up hanging out in his bed.) I finally had to face the facts when I found a cross necklace between the sheets and he told me it belonged to his friend Sarah. Sarah's Jewish."

WTF? *"After about a week of hanging out, I went over to this new guy's place, and there was a pair of girl's shoes and a cat toy by the door. I asked if he had a cat. He said he didn't. I asked why he had a cat toy if he didn't have a cat, and he made some awkward excuse that made no sense. Then I asked him whose shoes those were, and he said his sister had been* *helping him move in. I should have asked why his sister left her shoes at his house. Did she go home barefoot? Instead, I kept my mouth shut and went home at 3 A.M. with my panties in my purse. I found out a couple of days later that he was engaged to be married."*

He showers you with gifts.

While gifts are great—who doesn't love surprises?—if your guy suddenly becomes extra generous, it may be because he's trying to make up for his dishonest ways. The presents are less an apology than an attempt to assuage his own guilt, making him not only disloyal but also completely self-serving.

He's likely hoping that these gifts will overshadow your suspicions. Look out for things like out-of-the-blue jewelry when your guy has never previously shown an interest in buying you gems. Or he may get you expensive gifts that aren't really you, but more the kinds of items he thinks any typical girl would want—a dozen red roses instead of the lilies that are actually your favorite.

BIG RED-FLAG STORY:

"My boyfriend confessed to making out with another girl and, a week later while we were shopping, he bought me an expensive ring with a romantic inscription inside of it. While I was flattered that he'd purchase me something so pretty, every time I looked at the ring, which I wore every day at his prompting, I couldn't help but think about the real reason why he'd purchased it—because he felt guilty. So instead of being a sweet gift, the piece of jewelry simply reminded me of his infidelity. Not only that, but after said item was purchased, my boyfriend assumed I would be able to just forget about the fact that he'd broken my trust, as if the ring was supposed to fix everything. Sorry dude, doesn't work that way."

Nothing your cheating guy gives you will make up for the fact that he's giving the most important thing—his love and attention—to someone else. We say sell those presents on eBay and use the money to take a permanent vacay from this relationship.

His libido is MIA.

Even a man with a hearty sexual appetite will get full if he's overeating. If your guy's been busy gettin' busy with another lady, by the time he gets home to you there may not be enough wind in his sail to raise mast.

> *Red-Flag Rule #35:* If your vibrator is consistently serving as designated hitter, your man may be rounding the bases with another player, if you know what we mean.

Whether your guy might be gay, has morphed into a masturbating maniac (as we described in Chapters 4 and 9 respectively), or is screwing his secretary sideways, whenever a man turns you down for sex it hurts. You feel rejected, and rightfully so. But before you become self-conscious and wonder if it's something you did, confront your low-libido lover.

Ask him why sex seems to have been taken out of the relationship equation. He may point to stress, anxiety, or a change in medications. But if he doesn't head to the doctor to straighten these things out, there's a good chance the only medical condition he has is can't-keep-his-pants-on syndrome.

BIG RED-FLAG STORY:

"After being with my boyfriend for four years, and having a pretty consistent sex life, he started turning me down night after night. Sometimes he claimed to be tired, other times he said he was too full from dinner to have sex. He'd sleep on the other side of the bed, not cuddled up with me like he used to, and I swear that when I'd touch him, he'd literally flinch. He made it pretty obvious he wanted nothing to do with me physically. Due to that and other issues we were having (constant fights about nothing, general anger toward each other), we broke up. I found out from one of our mutual friends that he started dating—and sleeping with—this girl from college the week after we ended things. Apparently, they'd gotten pretty close during the last few months of our relationship and he sure didn't waste any time."

WTF? *"My friend's boyfriend habitually goes to this 'massage parlor' near his apartment where he pays $80 to get not just a happy ending, but full-on laid. While this is bad enough, I found out through one of his friends that the masseuses there don't make their clients wear condoms. And there have been times when he hasn't."*

He gushes about another woman.

Whether he can't shut up about his new coworker, yoga teacher, or supposed "friend," if your guy goes on and on about another woman, he could be guilty of emotional cheating and may not be far from physical cheating. His focus on this particular woman may start with a few short mentions and slowly graduate to extended conversations about everything from her career choice to her coffee choice.

BIG RED-FLAG STORY:

"My boyfriend has been 'friends' with a woman he's known for a long time. He frequently invites her and her husband over for dinner and she comes over without her husband half the time. When she's around, my boyfriend's eyes are glued to her and he's oblivious to me. She mentioned to him that she has cheated on her husband. I told him this situation makes me uncomfortable. (I've also recently noticed he's been very secretive about his texts and e-mails.) He says I'm being 'stupid' and 'jealous' that they're 'just friends' and says he absolutely will not change his friendship with her no matter how much it bothers me."

Relationships are about compromise: Your man shouldn't make you feel that giving up his female friendships is an unreasonable sacrifice if your comfort is at stake. When you confront him about his feelings for the one who seems to be his leading lady, he may tell you you're unreasonable and insist that he's allowed to have female friends.

However, in a marriage or even just a serious relationship, neither partner should actively seek new friendships with the opposite sex. Men and women are rarely capable of being "just friends" so your partner shouldn't take the risk of upsetting you, and if he does, clearly, he doesn't really love you. Besides, we'd be willing to bet your boyfriend's not okay, even in the slightest, with you striking up a friendship with that super hot guy at the gym.

He's not over his ex.

Red-Flag Rule #36: If right after you sleep with him, a guy tells you he feels guilty for having sex with you because he feels like he just cheated on his ex, put your clothes back on.

Even though he says he's dedicated to you, when a man's still hung up on his ex you're right to assume he'd sleep with her if given the chance. You guys may have a great relationship, but if he's not really over his last love, you can bet that the moment she hints that she wants him back, he'll be at her feet. The amount of time that's passed since he broke up with the girl in question is not always indicative of how "over" the relationship a guy is. If he still gushes about her or he can't hear her name without getting angry, watch out: He obviously has some strong feelings left for her, which will leave a sticky residue on your relationship.

BIG RED-FLAG STORY:
"I was dating this guy who constantly talked about his ex-girlfriend (seriously brought her up at least once an hour). I figured he was just trying to get over her and I didn't mind helping him along. Stupid, I know. Three months into the relationship he informed me that his ex wanted to get back together and he needed time to decide what to do. So he started dating both of us. Two weeks later, once I finally wised up and got sick of the situation, I found out that he was dating yet another girl the entire time."

However, a man doesn't need to actually want to get back with his ex to present a big red flag of the emotional cheating variety. If your guy is still hung up on, or hurting from, the last lady he loved, he's likely just not ready to give his heart to you. And no matter how great the guy seems, you'll always be sharing his affection with the ghost of another woman . . . sometimes literally.

WTF? *"I was about to go on my first date with this guy I just met, so, naturally, I Googled him just to make sure he wasn't a murderer* *or something. Imagine my surprise when I found a wedding-website-turned-obituary page for his dead fiancée, who had apparently passed away around a year ago. I was a little unsure about whether or not to go out with him after learning this information, because I was worried that he just got back out on the dating scene and maybe wasn't really over her. But I ended up deciding to go on the date because, a), he was a nice guy and, b), I couldn't tell him I looked him up.*

The date was really fun and, after too many whiskey sours, we decided to go back to his place. The next morning (when I was a little more observant) on my way to the bathroom I noticed framed engagement pictures all over the second floor of his flat. Then I saw that he still had her perfume out on the bathroom counter—it was the exact same perfume I wore. Freaked that he only liked me because I reminded him of—and smelled like—his lost love, I left quietly."

Red-Flag Rule #37: If a guy you're dating knows, to the day, how long he's been broken up with his ex, he's still in love with her.

THE BOTTOM LINE:

Women tend to believe the stories cheating men tell because we want to believe them. We're usually good at noticing these flags, but bad at coming to terms with them. Admitting that we're dating a two-timing twit forces us to question our judgment in men and worth as lovers, a process that tends to fuck with our heads and our hearts. But just like slowly pulling off a Band-Aid, dragging out the realization that your man's cheating only makes the hurt more painful in the end. Rip that sucker off quickly and the agony will be over before you know it.

WTF? *"I was already suspicious about my boyfriend because a bunch of things he said about himself, especially his past accomplishments and future endeavors, never quite checked out. So, when my boyfriend asked me to check his e-mail for him, I admit that I peeked at some of the chains. Turned out he was conversing with a few other 'girlfriends' (including his brother's wife), was hitting on one of my friends, and had five Internet dating accounts. No wonder he never got much sleep."*

Unfaithful men cheat because they need constant confirmation that more than one woman finds them worthy of affection. Don't let a scoundrel's hang-ups create a self-esteem issue for you—sure, you're more likely to proceed with caution in future relationships, but don't steer clear of intimacy altogether. Never letting another man in may prevent you from hurt, but it'll also prevent genuine love, leaving you lonely, jaded, and seriously praying for the extinction of the male species. Despite what the tabloids and Hollywood seem to say, there are good men out there who will treat your trust with the utmost care . . . and it's worth the risk to find one.

There will always be men who cheat, but you don't have to keep getting cheated on—if you notice a flag or your gut just tells you your man is a actually a manwhore, trust your instincts and flee the coop.

TOP TEN RED FLAGS:
Excuses He Gives for Not Being Able to See You

1. There's a *Gilmore Girls* marathon on tonight.
2. He's working on his toothpick castle.
3. He's in jail.
4. He has bad earwax buildup.

5. He promised to help bathe his friend's chinchilla.
6. His astrological chart says it's a bad day for love.
7. He's cleaning his gun.
8. His mom won't let him.
9. His great-uncle's stepmother's second cousin died.
10. He's too drunk.

Chapter Sixteen

He's a Control Freak

At first your guy's behavior might have been charming. He ordered for you on dates, warded off creepy guys at the bar, wanted to protect you. And what girl doesn't like being taken care of? However, no matter how much you like a man to dote on you, there's a distinction between him wanting what's best for you and deciding what's best for you.

> *Red-Flag Rule #38:* If your alleged knight in shining armor swoops in offering to improve every area of your life, he'll probably end up trying to control your life. Make sure he treats you like a princess, not like a project.

Controlling men's manipulative ways may take on a variety of forms: some guys berate you into being who they want you to be; some guys conquer by isolating you from your family and friends; some present ultimatums to run the relationship. Other men repeatedly "rescue" you—chipping away at your independence until you're fully dependent on them. Regardless, they are authoritarians who have a strong need to dictate. Dating one of these men puts you in an unhealthy situation, to say the least.

Controlling behavior is often excused as love and concern: Your boyfriend will say he's only acting jealous, calling constantly, and putting you down because he cares about you so much. For example, he disses your super-cute outfit, then tries to backpedal by saying he just doesn't want you to embarrass yourself in public.

Fact is, high-handed guys prey on women with low self-esteem who'll take their dominating actions as a form of flattery. Check out the following red flags, and if your guy's on a power trip fueled by his need for control, we suggest you flee ASAP.

It's his world (you're just living in it).

So your boyfriend's a bit picky: He likes his food prepared a certain way, his shirts hung in a certain order, and his newspaper read at a certain time. He's a man with a regimen and he's going to stick to the plan come hell or high water—bacon and eggs for dinner is not an option, tardiness is not acceptable, and forget about the chance for some impromptu afternoon sex. What he lacks in spontaneity he makes up for in stability. Which could be an admirable quality.

But when your man's idiosyncrasies impede on your freedom to be yourself and do as you please, and he expects you to live according to his rigid rules, you no longer have a peculiar guy with a few fixations on your hands—you have a full-blown control freak who can't have anything in his world out of order, especially not his girlfriend. If your guy commands you to follow his regime—er, regimen—remind him that he's not the emperor of your life.

BIG RED-FLAG STORY:

"My ex had so many superstitions, phobias, and things he just hated. He went crazy if I said 'fridge' instead of 'refrigerator,' and he hated Christmas so much he was actually fired from his job as a department store pianist because he refused to play Christmas songs around the holidays. There are dozens more examples, which might not have been problems had he under-stood that I didn't need to share his ridiculous rules. We finally broke up on Thanksgiving and as he was packing his stuff, I went shopping for Christmas decorations."

He makes all the decisions.

Like a stereotypical only child who doesn't know how to share, a controlling man makes it clear that your relationship is his way or the proverbial highway. From the restaurants you frequent to your sleeping arrangements, your man wants to be in charge or at least have final say. And if you don't like it, well, that's your problem. You can forget about your own needs and desires—he doesn't care. Unless, of course, you want what he wants, and, in that case, everything's good.

BIG RED-FLAG STORY:

"I love cuddling on the couch and watching TV with a guy, so I didn't mind that my ex wanted to stay in all the time. But we always had to watch what he wanted to, which was typically SportsCenter, and because we were almost always at his house, I didn't have a say. Whenever I mentioned that we should decide on something we both were interested in watching, his solution was for me to go into his bedroom where I'd have complete con-trol of the remote. Yeah, thanks . . . if I wanted to watch TV alone I would have just stayed home."

When your man is calling all the shots, ask yourself whether he likes you or the fact that you'll do whatever he wants. We assume you'd rather be a performer than a puppet, so you may need to find a different dude to act alongside you. Introduce him to the art of compromise: If he refuses to take turns, or does your thing but acts like a total dick the whole time, stop hanging with him and start hanging out alone—at least then you can do what you want.

He tells you how he expects you to behave.

A man who outlines, right off the bat, exactly how he expects you to perform the part of his girlfriend is more likely than not going to need to control everything in the relationship from how you act, to who you hang with, to what you think.

Natasha once went on a date with a guy her friends set her up with, and within the first half-hour of dinner he had already given her the rundown on how the courtship would go. He told her that he only calls a girl two times after a date—if she doesn't call him back, he'll delete her number. She couldn't help but feel like he was warning her not to be one of those girls, and while she appreciated him being up-front (not to mention the fact that he really was a good guy), maybe he could have waited at least until their food arrived to share these strict standards.

Control is a form of self-protection stemming from a lack of trust. If a man is in control of a situation—especially those of a romantic nature—he believes he can determine whether or not he gets hurt. Which is, of course, impossible. Risk is a part of any relationship. We all take risks with our hearts: Sometimes it works out, most of the time it doesn't, but you have to trust that it might or what's the point?

BIG RED-FLAG STORY:

"I recently went to a party with my girls and met a guy who was gorgeous. We hit it off and when I found out that he was an engineer, had his own apartment, and drove a fancy car, I was grateful to the dating gods for sending him my way.

"Just when I thought he couldn't get any better, all of a sudden he turned to me and said, 'Can I confess something? I think you are going to be my wife.' He proceeded to drill me with relationship questions like 'Have you ever cheated?,' 'What's the worst thing you've done to an ex?,' and my favorite, 'If I told you I felt uncomfortable with you going out with your friends, would you stay home with me and respect that?'

"Then he continued on with 'Can you promise to tell me you miss me throughout the day?' (Because, if I didn't, this would show that I had a lack of 'emotional sensitivity.') Seeing as I had only known this guy for an hour and a half at most, I decided to cut my losses."

He critiques everything you do.

Whether he thinks you're doing something wrong or he's just trying to keep you from "embarrassing yourself," controlling men will find ways to criticize your behavior, often under the guise of wanting to help you.

In relationships, critical men dominate by diminishing their partners. While they might not outright belittle or verbally abuse you, they have a way of making you feel inferior. A man may merely offer a suggestion, but say it with a slightly contemptuous tone, or teach you a new, "more efficient" way of doing something you've been doing every day for ten years (how you made it this far without him there to tell you how to wipe your own ass is a miracle).

BIG RED-FLAG STORY:
"Having dinner with a British guy I'd been dating for a few weeks, he took it upon himself to teach me how to eat properly. The conversation started with him asking me, 'Can I show you something?' I said sure. He proceeded to explain to me that Americans hold their silverware incorrectly, and that his way, i.e., the British way, was more polite, i.e., less offensive to him. After teaching me how to 'properly' hold my fork and knife, he told me that he wanted me to eat like that for the remainder of dinner. Feeling a little insecure, as you can imagine, I ate his way for the rest of the meal. At one point he even said, 'See, I told you it was easy, you're not even thinking about it.' Try again, buddy. Not only had I never felt so uncomfortable on a date, I never wanted to eat dinner with him again."

A micromanaging man chooses to express his superiority by being critical and patronizing. But if—God forbid—you offer a critique of something he does, wears, or says, he'll fly off the handle. The minute you start feeling insecure around a guy, walk away. Maintaining your self-worth can be hard enough; the last thing you need is a man whose ulterior motive is to keep you under his thumb.

He tells you what to do with your appearance.

Behind those backhanded comments about your weight and the occasional demand that you change into something "more appropriate" lies a control freak who will bend, break, and shape you to look like the woman he believes he deserves.

For example, we know a girl who met a guy online who wanted to buy her an outfit for her to wear on their first date. Sure, this gesture could be seen as sweet, but there's a point when a man's concern for your looks becomes obsessive, and his need for control takes on a form of ownership.

WTF? *"So this guy and I were really getting along, and having fun together doing normal, but very inexpensive, things. Then he announced that he wanted to do something nice for me—I started thinking that maybe he'll finally take me to a nice restaurant, or maybe we would even travel somewhere together. No. He wanted to buy me breast implants. And to be sure I knew this was a generous offer, he felt the need to tell me he'd done the same for his three previous girlfriends. Was I supposed to be flattered?"*

It's no secret that many women have body issues, and according to the National Eating Disorder Association, ten million women in the U.S. battle with some form of body-image-related condition. We have enough pressure from the media, from ourselves, from each other: Do we really need to hear from our boyfriends—men who are supposed to love us as we are—that our physiques aren't up to their standards?

As you constantly try to gain a controlling man's approval, believing he knows what's best for you, your self-confidence will slowly be eroded away, eventually leading you to conclude that you're not worthy of, nor would you ever be able to get, another man's attention. Feeling like you're stuck with your commanding guy makes you not just more dependent on him but even more willing to change yourself for him.

BIG RED-FLAG STORY:

"My former boyfriend and I joined a gym at the same time hoping that by doing it together we would start working out more regularly. He decided to sign up for personal training in addition to membership, as his bank account had more padding than mine. While that seemed like a really great idea, in that my boyfriend was going to get into crazy-good shape, his attitude toward me and my body totally changed after a couple of sessions. If he saw me eating pasta post-workout, he'd explain quite condescendingly that his trainer said not to eat carbs after cardio because it defeats the whole purpose. Given that I was 5 foot 4 and about 105 pounds at the time, his concern over my weight was ridiculous."

He doesn't support your interests outside of him.

Just like men who cheat, controlling men are typically quite insecure. They need you to need them and want to be the only person you turn to . . . for everything. Having a life outside of them is not an option—forget friends and often even family. Any strides you make toward your personal development will only be met by disdain. After all, he can't have you figuring out you're too good for him or anything.

> *Red-Flag Rule #39:* If your boyfriend tells you that you've changed since starting therapy, and he would like you to stop going, what he really means is that you've started standing up for yourself, and he would like you to stop.

BIG RED-FLAG STORY:

"After being at a dead-end job for five years, I decided that I wanted to go back to school for a Master's degree. I was super excited about the programs I was looking into and thought my boyfriend would be thrilled to see me so happy. Instead, he told me he didn't support me going back to school because if I got a degree I might eventually make more money than him, which apparently 'isn't how it's supposed to be.'"

A controller thinks the other people in your life will offer negative opinions of his behavior and influence your decision to be with him. He'll tell you these people treat you poorly, are using you, or simply don't understand the love you share with him. If you hang out with your friends, he'll give you the third degree, prompting you to conclude that it's simply not worth having other relationships if you'll be forced to suffer his consequences. Once he's distanced you from the other people in your life, he can assert even more control, pointing out that if it weren't for him, you'd be completely alone.

WTF? *"My ex hated that I would go out with my girlfriends because 'people in relationships don't go out.' After we broke up, he would send me thirty text messages in a row, calling in between. I even tried to tell him that I had cheated on him just so he would get over me. I ended up having to change my number, but I still receive e-mails from him—in which he makes sure to let me know how much better looking he is than my new boyfriend."*

He toys with your emotions.

One minute you're hot and heavy, the next the guy says he needs some space. Controlling men mess with your head like a drug does: The initial flood of serotonin and that rush of incredible feelings hook you, then the guy administers just enough love and attention to keep you coming back. When he withholds his emotions, you experience withdrawal and your need for him grows even stronger.

You may find yourself caught in a cycle of sweet/mean or infatuated/uninterested: one day your man's doting and the next he's distant, then before you know it he's all about you again. You hold on in the hopes that each cycle will be the last and that the nice version of him will become the only one. Instead, he'll more likely continue to build you up then break you down until you're so shattered that all the king's horses and all the king's men won't be able to put you back together again.

Any relationship founded on a game of emotional tug of war is bound to land you face first in the mud. Tell him how his behavior makes you feel, and if he acts like he couldn't care less if you dropped off the face of the earth, take him up on it and disappear from his life forever.

BIG RED-FLAG STORY:

"I began dating a guy I'd been good friends with for a long time. After about nine months, and given that we were both in our early thirties, things started getting serious. He sat me down one day and said we were moving too fast and he wasn't sure if he could 'do this anymore.' My first instinct was to just break up, but I really thought we had something, so I asked him to please give it some time and I would try to give him more space. He said okay.

"Three months later, same story. We were getting too close, he said, and it was 'scaring' him how much he 'felt for me.' We broke up. While I was devastated, I decided to just move on and try to get over it. I told him not to contact me—that I would call him when I was ready and maybe we could try to be friends again. A month passed without contact and I ended up meeting another guy who was really sweet and seemed to have the same priorities I did regarding relationships.

"As soon as my ex saw I had moved on, he started calling me, begging me to come back to him. But he didn't just call me like a normal person would: He called my cell phone. I didn't answer. He texted me. I didn't respond. He called my work phone. I didn't pick it up. He even tried to trick me by calling my company's main line and having our receptionist patch him through. (Which I accidentally answered, not thinking he would do that.) Then he sent me flowers. It was so obvious that he only wanted me as soon as he couldn't have me."

He uses your love for him against you.

In Chapter 11, we covered men who use your desire to please them in bed to sucker you into sexual acts you're not comfortable with. Similarly, controlling men will use your love to guilt you into doing whatever they want both inside and outside the bedroom. A man should never use your feelings as leverage: His willingness to exploit your emotions for his personal gain shows he's selfish and doesn't give two shits about how he's affecting you. If your guy starts using statements like "If you really love me, you'd do x," that's a cue that he actually doesn't love you. Next time he feeds you that line, feed it right back to him: "If you really love me, you'll stop using my love as barter."

BIG RED-FLAG STORY:

"Once, when I was young, stupid, and desperate, I begged my then boyfriend not to break up with me by giving in to his various requests—all of which would signal (in his opinion) that I really loved him. After promising all sorts of things from not getting mad at him, to cooking for him, to lowering my expectations, he finally agreed to stay with me."

He hurts himself to get your attention.

We've heard horror stories from girls whose boyfriends threatened to kill themselves when and if their relationships ended. And we've received similar submissions from women through our blog. Such acts of desperation are incredibly manipulative and completely self-serving. While a man may be so heartbroken he can't imagine going on, he shouldn't treat his life like a negotiating asset for getting you back.

A controlling man may even purposefully hurt himself or feign sickness just to get your attention. He's not desperate to stay with you; he's desperate to control you, even if it means losing a leg (literally). If you genuinely think your man will harm himself, speak with his family and get him professional help. But if you're certain he's just using threats to get what he wants, this behavior might signal another kind of serious mental instability.

BIG RED-FLAG STORY:

"When the guy I had just started dating told me he had emotional issues and that he was bipolar, I was a little taken aback that he shared such personal information so soon. However, I wasn't going to judge him for a condition he couldn't help, and since he was on medication I didn't think it was an issue.

"Fast-forward a few months. I had just moved into a new house and was busy one night assembling my bedroom furniture when he kept texting me to find out when we were going to hang out. I told him maybe later, and that I had to finish my room first. He then texted me four more times, at which point I asked that he stop bothering me because I wanted to get my stuff done.

"A half hour later, he called to tell me that he was going to the hospital because his medication was 'messed up.' Worried,

I rushed to the emergency room and ran into his sister in the lobby. She asked me if we were fighting earlier and I told her what had happened over the course of the night. Then she asked if I thought he had done this on purpose. When I had the chance to talk to him alone I asked him if he had knowingly screwed up his meds. He had. As it turned out, it was my job as his girlfriend to constantly appease him so that he didn't purposefully overdose for attention."

WTF? *"My boyfriend was upset that I wasn't spending enough time with him so he faked being in a car accident. He said he was okay but had some bumps/bruises and was gonna be stuck in bed for a few days. I felt really, really bad and immediately went over to his place, stopping on the way to pick up some DVDs I thought would cheer him up. I arrived to find him playing beer pong with some buddies. He hadn't been in a car accident. He just wanted to 'see how much I loved him.'"*

He basically wants a mail-order bride.

There's something a little scary about men who talk about wanting a girlfriend without having a real-life girl in mind. It's like they want someone to take care of and protect, but don't really care who that person is. We like to call this the "insert girl here" scenario, and we're not fans.

This man rules his life plan with an iron fist and needs to make sure it all pans out as planned . . . that's where you come in. When a guy's just looking for a girl, any girl, to take on the role of his future wife, he already has a clear picture of how that role should be played. Instead of getting to know a woman, he equates her with this fictional character and expects her to give the performance of a lifetime. When, a few months into the relationship, she breaks character, he feels betrayed and wants to know what happened to the girl he fell in love with. Umm . . . she doesn't exist and never did.

Think about how much effort your man puts into getting to know the details of your life and personality. Did your beau ask personal questions about your past, family, and future goals at the start of the relationship? Does he still do so now? If you answered no to both of those questions, it's possible that he doesn't love you, but just the idea of you. Find a man who wants to date a person, not an impersonation, or you'll eventually find yourself living the life of someone you don't know and never intended to be.

BIG RED-FLAG STORY:

"When I was on the second date with a guy, he told me that he wanted to bring me to his mother's house. Then he mentioned how great his married friends had said it was to be married. To top it off, he threw in that he'd switch his religion to mine if we got married. He wasn't joking or laughing about it, either. After that second date, it was definitely over. The guy wasn't looking for a girlfriend, he was looking for a mail-order bride."

THE BOTTOM LINE:

Whether he's jealous, chauvinistic, or just plain insecure, there's no excuse for a man who exhibits controlling behavior. A healthy relationship consists of respect and support, not one person calling all the shots. Even if he says he'll change, he probably won't—cut your losses before you lose your sense of self, sense of worth, and sense of right and wrong.

> *Red-Flag Rule #40:* If he's not just taking the reins, but strangling you with them, knock him off his high horse before your heart gets trampled.

There's a very strong link between controlling behavior and physical abuse, so get out of a controlling relationship before it becomes dangerous not just for your mental health but also for your physical well-being. The longer you let a guy control you, the less likely you are to leave him. The less likely you are to leave him, the more damaged you'll ultimately end up.

TOP TEN RED FLAGS:
Signs He's Turning to 'Roids

1. He visits you during your lunch break and makes you oil him up.
2. When you don't get the protein-fat-carb ratio right, he accuses you of being involved in a giant conspiracy to make him chubby.
3. Big and Tall doesn't make a neck big enough for him.
4. When you catch him flexing in public he says, "It's what people want to see."
5. He has more drugs in his cabinets than CVS.
6. His voice starts sounding like James Earl Jones's.
7. He suddenly has acne worse than the "befores" on a Proactiv commercial.
8. He sets up Strong Man obstacle courses in the yard.
9. His balls look like prunes.
10. He rubs the blood from his frequent nosebleeds all over his face while shouting lines from *Braveheart*.

CONTROLLING BEHAVIOR, much like cheating, using, and refusing to commit, shows how a guy is more concerned with himself than he is with you. While your guy not being ready to propose isn't as malicious as him sleeping with your best friend, at their core, the flags in this section indicate how a guy is not at the point in his life where he's willing to put other people's needs and desires—namely yours—before his own.

Red-Flag Case Study #4

See how many red flags you can spot in just one story:

One day, I found a text on my boyfriend's phone from an unsaved number that read: "Today was fun . . . spontaneous. Are you not available tonight?" I called the number and a girl answered. When I confronted him about it, he claimed his friend had borrowed his phone in order to text girls.

I found two more texts in the outbox addressed to the same number. One was titled "ME" with a photo of my boyfriend, and it was followed by a second text reading, "I wood love to cum see you!" (Yes, written exactly like that.) When I confronted my boyfriend, he said he sent those messages to everyone in his phone by accident when he was drunk, and that he also accidentally sent everyone a picture of me in my bikini as well. (Great.)

The next night I heard him come home around 2 A.M. after he was out drinking. He turned his phone off before getting into bed. The next morning I woke up and he was still sleeping, so I checked his phone. Sure enough, he'd sent another text to the same number: "R U up? If so let me make you cum!" I woke up the friend who supposedly borrowed my boyfriend's phone (he was sleeping on our couch), and demanded that he recite the number the text was sent to, tell me who it was to, and word-for-word what it said without speaking with my boyfriend—or I was moving out. He did all of those things and said he was the one texting. My boyfriend and I have been together for two years, live together, and there are no other signs of infidelity.⚑

⚑ He's shady. But so is she—and she must have been already having doubts.

⚑ He's like super shady.

⚑ How can the photo be of his friend if the person in it actually is her boyfriend?

⚑ He makes us want to vomit in our mouths. Yuck. The guy sounds like a thirteen-year-old.

⚑ He's immature and disrespectful. If a guy does really dumb things that also affect you when he's drunk, there's a problem.

⚑ He acts like he's single. Guys in relationships can go out with their "boys," but why is he constantly partying without her?

⚑ He's most certainly cheating.

Part Five

He's Just the Worst

Chapter Seventeen

He Has the Worst Life

Some men are just, in Julie's words, "the worst." While the three of us initially thought this was an indefinable categorization—and simply a reflex repulsion brought on by dating certain men—we were able to pinpoint what characteristics make a guy earn this distinction, the first of which are related to the state of his life in general.

Relationships mesh two people's lives: You invite the guy you're dating into your personal affairs and in return he shares his private world with you. This doesn't mean that each of you compromises your own independence merely because you've decided to couple; it does mean, however, that how your boyfriend chooses to live his life impacts yours.

> *Red-Flag Rule #41:* If the guy you're dating tells you he can't commit to a relationship right now because he's "processing a lot," don't wait around for him to work through his shit. We're *all* processing a lot . . . it's called life.

You could be dating the sweetest, most romantic guy on earth, but if he's living in a dumpster, waiting to be discovered by a Hollywood producer, chances are the relationship's not going to work out. Or the most successful, sought-after bachelor in New York City could be courting you, but if he has to entertain clients at happy hour five days a week and spends his weekends golfing with potential contacts, you and the relationship will undoubtedly be neglected.

Whether or not the guy in question is officially your boyfriend or someone you just met, before you rearrange your life to accommodate a relationship with him, you should take inventory of his life. After all, if your main man's life is just the worst, yours will eventually suck, too.

He has the worst past and won't shut up about it.

Before we get to men whose current situations are the worst, we need to address those who have everything they've ever wished for, or at the very least lead pretty damn good lives, but refuse to enjoy them because they're hung up on their woe-is-me histories. A guy like this will lament his painful past and point to it as the root of every single problem—from why he lacks confidence to why he gets cavities. In his daily life, all roads lead to twenty years ago when his dad left the family or when he was teased about his back brace in elementary school.

There's no point, nor is it any fun, dating a man who chooses to be victimized by his past. No one's childhood was perfect—at least no one we know, anyway. But as adults we can decide to either continue to play the victims and be miserable or work through our pasts in order to enjoy the present. You won't be able to appreciate your life if you're too busy hearing about, and comforting him over, his.

BIG RED-FLAG STORY:
"I knew a guy in college who would relate every conversation you had with him back to his shitty upbringing. You mention

how you're craving a hamburger; he'd lament about the time his mom tried to buy him a Happy Meal with food stamps. You say your dad's coming to visit this week; he'd retort he was glad his dad was dead so he couldn't beat up his mom anymore. It was really sad, but also really annoying. We were in a class together where we were supposed to write personal essays, and one girl (who was really nice and outgoing) told the story of how she and her family escaped a civil war in Africa. I have no idea how she sat there the whole time, not saying anything, as the poor-me guy complained about what a shitty time he had every two seconds, while she had been through much, much worse."

A lot of women seem to be turned on by damaged dudes because they're mysterious and challenging. We feel empowered by the promise of being able to save a broken beau by offering him a happy future to make up for his sucky past. But what you have to realize is that a grown man who's caught up feeling sorry for himself because his past wasn't so peachy doesn't want to be saved.

Having a dude depend on you may make you feel needed, but when you invest so much energy in your boyfriend, you often ignore your own problems, feelings, and needs, which become subordinate to his in the relationship—which is why we don't recommend getting involved with a man who has clearly not healed from his past. Whether he likes the attention or his identity is wrapped up in playing the victim, it's not your job to make him see the light.

He's a workaholic.

While you don't want a man with no direction or drive, we're not sure being in a relationship with a work-obsessed, no-time-to-play Jack is a healthy situation either. Having a relationship with a workaholic can be very challenging, and you may often feel slighted when your guy chooses his need to succeed over his desire to be with you. But it's not personal. And clearly, you can't expect him to change his deep-rooted ways just because you decided to come along.

Instead, you need to ask yourself what you're willing to compromise. If you're the type of gal who enjoys her independence and relishes her free time, dating a workaholic might be an ideal situation for you. On the other hand, if you're slightly more needy and can't fathom why your boyfriend's work comes before your relationship, dating an overachiever is only going to lead to record-level resentment.

Either way, you need to understand that workaholics are addicts—your man's need to work will control his every impulse. And no matter how much you love him, or he loves you . . . you, my dear, will never come before his addiction.

BIG RED-FLAG STORY:
"My friend's dad is the head of a really large company and pretty much has more money than God. However, he barely sees his family—he lives in the city five days a week (and sometimes weekends too, if he's working), while they live about two hours away, in another state. Even though he could totally retire, and probably could have a decade ago, spend time with his kids and grandkids, and travel the world with his wife, he continues to work long hours and make excuses for why he needs to continue to do so."

He's up to some shady business.

Unless he's some sort of secret agent working for the CIA, any guy who "can't tell you" what he does for a living isn't doing anything you want any part of. Your boyfriend may have "personal invest-ments" on the side, a.k.a. he's laundering money for the mob, or he may be an "entrepreneur" (who happens to deal in cash only), a.k.a. he's selling meth to high school kids. It doesn't matter. If your man's up to some shady business, don't be surprised when his bookie's muscle shows up to break your legs, too.

Scary implications aside, being in a relationship with a man who hides his day-to-day dealings will be frustrating, to say the least. Trust will be an issue because he'll never be able to tell you the whole truth, and you'll end up having to lie to your friends and family about your guy's profession, among other things. As you continue to mimic your crooked dude's behavior, you'll end up just as shady as him.

BIG RED-FLAG STORY:
"While talking intimately with this guy at a bar multiple people (mainly men) kept coming up to him and interrupting our con-versation. At first I thought, okay, he knows everybody here, this must be his Friday night spot. But then when we were outside around the corner making out, and guys were still approaching him, I became a little more suspicious. Why would so many peo-ple at the club urgently insist on speaking to him? Two words: drug dealer."

He's just a loser.

Three years into the relationship and your guy's still doing the same old thing, which in this case is nothing. He's going nowhere at a lethargic pace, and he's not the least bit concerned about it. In fact, he's perfectly content living in his grandma's garage, working part-time at the head shop, and getting stoned for breakfast.

Sorry to break it to you, though we suspect you've realized it: Your boyfriend's a loser. Dropped out of college, can't hold a job, doesn't have a car, lives at his parents', never takes you out, has no plans for the future, spends his afternoons drinking forties and playing "asshole" with his asshole friends, who are, of course, unemployed with nowhere to be either. (Perhaps your man surrounds himself with these fellow deadbeats so his empty-headed existence doesn't seem so bad.)

The good news is that you don't have to be a part of your guy's worthless world. Even if you think he's got potential, it's not your responsibility to make sure he lives up to it. Sticking around until he does may leave you in financial and emotional debt. (Besides, chances are if he's twenty-eight and hasn't had a full-time job since . . . ever, his prospects are meager at best.)

You, after all, have your shit together. He, by contrast, has nothing to offer you. In fact, he can't even remember to pick up toilet paper, like you asked, when it was the only thing he had to accomplish all day. This irresponsible, unmotivated mess of a man will also make a mess of your life if you hold on to the hope that he'll wake up and make something of himself. Never going to happen.

BIG RED-FLAG STORY:

"The first and only time I hung out with this dude he revealed that while on probation for drug charges, he had been caught with a fake penis full of someone else's urine in an attempt to pass a pee test required by the terms of said probation. When he told me that he takes care of his sick father, I thought maybe he was a good person who had made a few wrong choices. However, what he really meant was that he merely lived in his sick father's basement. His 'boy,' who was recently released from jail on bail, also lived in his sick father's basement.

"Needless to say, I was not enamored. After I ignored his calls and texts for the next few weeks, he defriended me on Facebook and I thought that was the end of it. But no. He began messaging me via MySpace to let me know that he didn't get why I was blowing him off. When I told him it was because he was a 'druggie and criminal,' he accused me of having 'high expectations.'"

He's using the system.

Deadbeats of the loser and shady-business variety often have an unfounded sense of entitlement. Instead of pulling up their boots by the straps and taking charge of their lives like men, they complain about the way things are in attempts to justify their dubious actions (or inactions). They're the victims and life's the culprit.

Because of this, they feel justified in taking advantage of the government programs put in place to help those who're seriously down and out by using the much-needed resources to improve their own lives. Unemployment, worker's compensation, welfare, you name it—your guy screws Uncle Sam so he doesn't have to actually work for the American Dream.

Asking for government help by doing things like filing for unemployment in itself isn't necessarily a red flag. However, a grown man's decision to collect checks made with your tax dollars, while he continues to contribute nothing to society, is.

BIG RED-FLAG STORY:
"I dated this guy who told me he was a successful photographer. In actuality, he faked an injury to go on disability leave from his regular job so he could spend more time on his 'photography business' (i.e., he and his buddies getting stoned and taking terrible pictures)."

He's in the system.

We're going to go out on a limb and say that if your boyfriend's currently in prison, he has the worst life. No judgment—none of us have pined for a man behind bars—but why any girl would continue a relationship with a convicted felon is beyond us. Yet it happens: Women are loyal to the men they love, even if said men won't see daylight outside the prison courtyard for fifteen years. Your best bet is to either not fall in love with a man who you suspect is up to no good or be willing to say goodbye (through a Plexiglas window) upon his conviction.

A WORD ON
Ex-Con Rehabilitation

According to the Federal Bureau of Justice, three years after being released from jail, two-thirds of ex-cons are rearrested and one half are reincarcerated. Most prisoners leave the slammer with pocket money, a bus ticket, and, if they have kids, child-support debts. With employment difficult to find, and parole fees piling up, this dude will need significant financial help. Who you date is your choice, but just know exactly what you're getting into before committing to a former felon.

Knowingly becoming involved with a recent ex-con just isn't in your best interests. First, you'll have to take the crime the guy committed into account. Then there's also the fact that he'll have a bumpy road ahead to re-establish himself as a civilian, which we'd argue should be his first priority, not dating you. He also may not be able to function in society—employment, insurance, and loans, among other things, will be hard for him to secure. Plus, one slip-up and he's back in the slammer . . . and then you're in for conjugal visits.

BIG RED-FLAG STORY:

"I was dating a guy and things were going great. All of a sudden, I stopped hearing from him—he didn't pick up my calls, wouldn't respond to my Facebook messages, etc. So I moved on. A month and a half later I got a letter in the mail from him with 'Correctional Facility' stamped on the front. He was in prison for armed robbery. His letter said he missed me and he knows that I'm 'the one' for him."

While love's often worth taking risks for, dating a guy with a criminal past may put you in enough danger to negate this notion. Seriously consider how his circumstances will affect your relationship—as well as your life outside the relationship—before getting in too deep to dig your way out.

WTF? *"After my divorce, I was slow to re-enter the dating scene because I hadn't been a part of it for almost twenty years. My friend convinced me to go on a double date with a guy she'd been out with once before and his friend. I knew nothing about the friend but thought a double date would be a nice way to ease back into things.*

"When our guys arrived, I noticed that mine was a little rough around the edges, but didn't want to be judgmental. I mentioned that I hadn't been on a date in a long time and he replied that he hadn't either. I asked if he was newly divorced too and he said no 'but I just got out of prison after twelve years . . . today.'

"His friend, and my friend's date, had picked him up at jail that afternoon; they came pretty much straight from prison to the restaurant. I was hoping he'd at least been in for some sort of white-collar crime, but no, he was in for kidnapping."

He has five baby mamas.

Dating a dude with kids is a very personal decision, and not one that should be made lightly. For starters, the relationship will never be solely between you and your beau—there will always be a third (or fourth or fifth or sixth) party to consider. Should you become an integral part of the family unit, you will have to deal with them on a daily basis.

But in addition to having your life revolve around another woman and his children with her, how your guy deals with these children speaks volumes about who he is. A guy who makes babies but doesn't raise children is irresponsible. Don't believe him when he says that if you got pregnant it would be different. If he's got six kids with five women you can't really trust his word.

Think about if and how he makes his children a priority: Any dude who's more interested in whisking his hottie girlfriend (uh, that's you, honey) off to Cancun than seeing his child perform in the Christmas play is not someone you should aim for a future with. If he makes no effort to have his kids in his life, he's probably too self-involved to make sacrifices not just for them, but for you as well.

BIG RED-FLAG STORY:

"I began dating a guy I met online and he told me on our first date that he had never been married. This couldn't have been farther from the truth: He actually was married (separated from his wife) and had not one but two kids. (And I actually didn't find out the 'married' part until much, much later. He told me his kids were with his 'baby mama'—but that's a whole other story.)

"Before he confessed to having kids (I say confessed, but really, he only told me when I caught him in one of his many lies), he would apparently hide all of his photos of them in his house and give up his time with them so he could take me out. I even spotted a car seat in his garage and when I asked him about it, told me it was for his 'niece' in case his sister visited. While the lying to me was bad enough, the real flag for me was how this guy could completely pretend he wasn't a dad—a real man would have been proud to be a father."

THE BOTTOM LINE:
The state of a man's life is a reflection of the man himself. On the surface, he could seem like the most amazing guy ever, but take a closer look at his day-to-day dealings and you might just discover a world you have no interest in exploring—or at least shouldn't for the sake of your mental and emotional health.

WTF? *"While on a blind date with someone I met online, I asked him if he had any crazy/funny blind date stories. He must have misunderstood my question, thinking I asked if he had ever done anything crazy/funny with someone he was dating. He replied, 'I trashed someone's apartment once. My girlfriend, I was mad at her and went over to her apartment when she wasn't there and trashed the place. But this was almost ten years ago.' Hmm . . . anything else you want to tell me, buddy? 'Well,' he said, laughing, 'I once sort of held my girlfriend hostage for two to three hours. I just had a lot to say and needed her to listen. This was a long time ago, though.'"*

When you're in a relationship with someone, you not only put yourself in a position to share dinners, movies, and your time in general with him, you're gearing up to potentially share your lives (and pasts). Along the way, you're both certain to have turbulent times, and a strong couple will help each other cope. But if your man's entire life is a rough patch, smoothing it out will take tons of time, patience, and energy. While fixing his life, you could ignore and simultaneously screw up your own.

Again, timing counts for a lot here: You could meet the seemingly perfect guy but he may not be in a good place in his life to adequately be your partner. Of course, his circumstances don't automatically make him a bad person, but they could make him the wrong person for you, for now. Relationships work best when both people have their own lives under enough control to add someone else to the mix.

TOP TEN RED FLAGS:
His Chosen Career

1. Nursing home pimp
2. Motivational speaker: "Positive Thinking and the Power of Colonics"
3. Carny
4. Janitor at a happy-ending massage parlor
5. Self-described "healer"
6. Blogger for tittytwist.com
7. Strip club deejay
8. President of The Official Fellatio Fan Club
9. Philosopher (no degree, no books, no audience, but it's the title in his e-mail signature)
10. Flatulence expert

Chapter Eighteen

He Has the Worst Family

Every family has its quirks. But, for some reason, other people's families—including your man's—often seem to have way more than your own. Since you're used to how your family takes vacations, celebrates the holidays, or simply just hangs out together (or doesn't), adapting to your guy's tribe might take time. However, there's a difference between a fam that's eccentric and one that's deranged. We can excuse the family that wears matching outfits to Christmas dinner, but not the one that wears their birthday suits to Sunday brunch.

If you plan to marry your guy someday, or even if you're planning to date him for a while, you should size up his family as you did him. In addition to how they treat each other, pay attention to how they treat you—just as your man should show you love and respect, his family should too, making you feel, in turn, like a welcome addition, not an unwanted outgrowth.

Red-Flag Rule #42: If the family tree is rotten, the apple that falls from it will be, too: Your guy's relatives' behavior and interactions reveal who he really is and explain how he got that way.

Of course, you can't assume that your man is going to turn out exactly like the rest of his family, and it's probably not a good idea to preemptively judge him as such—we know plenty of dudes with a-hole dads who are lovely gentlemen. Still, any man is the product of the environment he was raised in, and though he may not totally take on all of his parents' morals and values, he was certainly influenced by them. Even if your boyfriend claims he's nothing like the rest of his gang, his relatives may be the people you'll end up spending holidays and celebrations with for the rest of your life. More importantly, they're the ones you'll raise your kids around.

While we don't think the point of every relationship is necessarily to procreate, the truth of the matter is that many of us still operate under the notion that dating leads to marriage, which leads to kids. So, if you're with the majority on this progression, it is indeed important to measure a man not just as a lover but also as a father. While you and your guy need not have been raised similarly, you should agree on how to bring up your children, a determination heavily influenced by how you and your man were brought up. No matter what, his family will affect you and your relationship.

His family is really dysfunctional.

We have yet to meet a group of related people who talk about their issues calmly and constructively without the help of a therapist. Some families work out their problems by yelling at one another. Others prefer the passive-aggressive-silent-treatment method. The completely "functional" family doesn't exist, as far as we can tell.

That said, if joining your guy's family for dinner feels more like a mediation, where the tension hangs so thick you could cut it with a knife, or the atmosphere is louder than a boxing match because of the constant shouting and pounding of fists upon the table, you'll need to evaluate whether that's the kind of ambiance you want to dine in for the long term.

One of our blog submitters shared a story about how her guy's mother was an outrageously emotional, self-involved person who was prone to blowing up over something completely random. For example, if the rest of the family didn't feel like eating at the restaurant she wanted to go to for dinner, this woman would lock herself in her bedroom until one of her kids—usually the girl's boyfriend—would go in there and persuade her to come out. Sometimes this convincing took hours. This was not the type of woman she wanted her hypothetical kids to call Grandma one day. (And she was a little worried about the fact that her boyfriend felt obligated to continually cater to his drama queen of a mother, whom he often defended. Only a momma's boy would make allowances for that kind of behavior.)

It's important to watch how your man interacts with his parents and siblings in particular. While he may reinforce their bad behavior, as in the example above, he may also simply treat them like crap. If he puts his family members down, teases them to the point of being cruel, or screams at them in front of you, we'd hate to see how he treats them behind closed doors. And we'd really be worried to see how he acts toward your family, given the environment he's used to.

> *Red-Flag Rule #43:* If a guy treats his mother like dirt, it's very likely he'll treat you terribly, too.

The rule above goes for grandmothers as well: Meagan's ex refused to bring flowers to his soon-to-die grandmother on Mother's Day because it was Mother's Day, not Grandmother's Day. She pointed out that the holiday was in celebration of all mothers and that she was bringing a card to her own grandma. He responded conde-scendingly, as if Meagan was an idiot for confusing her mother with her grandmother. This caused a fight, and she realized she never wanted to be the mother of his children because she'd never get a day of thanks, Mother's Day or otherwise, for birthing their off-spring because she wasn't his mother.

BIG RED-FLAG STORY:
"The first time I met my now ex-boyfriend's mom, I went to din-ner with him, her, his two brothers, and one of his brothers' girl-friends. During dinner his mother and brothers ended up getting into an argument, causing her to scream at them and storm away from the table. Twice. In the middle of a crowded restaurant. Apparently this was normal operative procedure for this family.

"Needless to say, this behavior left a deep impression. Of course, not deep enough for me to stop dating the guy right then, but I certainly took my ex's mother's antics into consideration when I later broke up with him."

His family has no boundaries.

Like discovering fifty dollars in an old pair of jeans, finding a guy who comes from a loving and functional family is freaking phenom-enal. You don't absolutely need to love your guy's clan, but if you do, it's a definite bonus. Any boyfriend who is close to his siblings and parents—regularly talking to them on the phone, taking vacations together, supporting one another in general—gets a major gold star.

But there is such a thing as family members who are just a bit too close for comfort. Some families really have no boundaries or inhibitions at all. Which is fine . . . until their unusual actions start to weird you out.

For example, we know a girl who literally had to beg her boyfriend to put on clothes when he stayed with her family during the holidays. In the morning, he would walk from her bedroom to the bathroom (which she shared with her little brother) in just his boxers, with his hairy chest—and potentially his package—exposed to whoever happened to be in the hallway. Her parents aren't super conservative, but they wear clothes, especially when they have guests. One time he even tried coming down for breakfast in just his underwear, thinking that would be totally cool. She realized when she visited his family why he thought this was normal: His dad lounged around in his boxers—completely not caring that his son's girlfriend could pretty much see his penis.

While most families do cover their genitals, some keep everything else out in the open, specifically their thoughts and emotions, no matter how off-color or inappropriate. There aren't many topics of conversation that catch us off guard, but if a guy we're dating casually mentions doing lines of coke with his mom during his effed-up childhood, as one blog submitter of ours shared, we're going to be a bit uncomfortable. Here's the distinction: It's nice when a brother and sister can chat about the details of their respective lives. It's creepy when a brother and sister can chat about the details of their respective sex lives.

BIG RED-FLAG STORY:
"I spent one New Year's Eve with my boyfriend at his parents' house. Since the place was literally on a mountain, and it was snowing, we decided not to venture out but instead to just flip on the TV for a couple of hours and watch the ball drop. After we'd changed into pajamas, I figured we would go into what was 'our room' to do this.

"My boyfriend, however, thought we should go watch reruns of *Law and Order* with his mom and dad in their room until it got closer to midnight. But we couldn't sit on the leather loveseat next to their bed, or on the floor. No, my boyfriend insisted we literally get in his parents' bed, with them. Under the covers. I didn't know what else to do, so I climbed in, too (even though his dad was just in his boxer shorts). No one had a problem with this. In fact, at one point, I looked over to find my boyfriend spooning his mom."

WTF? *"My ex-boyfriend lived with his older brother. (They were both in their early twenties.) On the nights I didn't spend at their place, they would sleep in the same bed. And, if his brother's girlfriend was over, my boyfriend would climb into bed with both of them."*

His family puts him on a pedestal.

Whether he's an only child, the first-born, or just the favorite, beware of the family who thinks your man is God's gift to the world. Not only will their constant praising of his every action get annoying (no matter how proud of him you are), but it's quite likely that no woman will ever be good enough for their little savior.

BIG RED-FLAG STORY:

"I dated a guy for three years and every holiday, birthday, or occasion in which gifts were given, his parents would give me framed photos of him as a baby. Okay, one framed picture was cute, two was slightly repetitive, but eighteen and you've got yourself one hell of a momma's boy and one set of seriously child-obsessed parents who will always see you as a threat."

If your dude recognizes his fam's tendency to treat him like king and you two can laugh about it after visits with them, that's totally fine. But if he either doesn't discern the situation or seems to actually need the praise to stroke his ego, it may signal either an inflated sense of self-importance or a problem with self-confidence, possibly both.

Even if the guy isn't a total egomaniac after all that constant adoration, the way his parents treat him can create an unhealthy situation for you as his family constantly reinforces your inferiority to him. Not only are these people likely to scrutinize your every move, but we worry they will take issue with your parenting approach when you have kids—or worse, they will treat your children with the same disciple-like devotion they've given their son.

His family continually compares you to his ex.

In this case, the issue isn't that no woman will ever be good enough for your man. In fact, there's someone who is perfect for him . . . it's just not you. It's the one who got away.

Aside from the insecurities that will no doubt creep in upon hearing all about how so-and-so was amazingly cute or talented or kind or super-smart, this kind of comparing is just plain rude. And if your guy isn't willing to stand up to his folks and tell them they'd better stop dissing his new darling, you shouldn't be willing to stay with him and endure his family's praising of his long-lost love.

BIG RED-FLAG STORY:

"I once dated a dude who had a devout Catholic upbringing. I wasn't raised religious; his family knew this and hated it about me. They wanted me to believe exactly what they did. His last girlfriend apparently went to Mass with them every Sunday, something they constantly made known to me just to show how inadequate of a match I was for their son."

His family doesn't treat you like you're one of them.

Sure, your dude's mom isn't going to drape you in the family jewels the moment your guy introduces you, but his parents should make an effort to make you feel comfortable and, at the very least, include you, when you spend time with them. If they're going to invite you to be with the family, they should treat you as if you're part of it. It's just the right thing to do.

If your guy's family is cold, their standoffish behavior raises some questions: Do they actually know you're his girlfriend? Does your guy go through girlfriends like boxers and his folks aren't getting to know you because they assume you'll be tossed out soon? Do they think blood relatives are more worthy than those who marry into the family? Are they just distant, unfriendly people? No matter what the answers are, by treating you like an outsider, they are giving you the clear signal that you may never break into their inner circle.

Tell your boyfriend that he needs to get his family on board or you're abandoning ship. When his family's ill treatment of you does not upset him, he's either a wuss who refuses to stand up to his surly tribe or he doesn't care enough about you. The End.

BIG RED-FLAG STORY:

"One year, I hand-made Christmas presents for my serious boyfriend's entire family. When I went with my guy to spend the holidays with them, I passed out my gifts and they gave me nothing in return. (Money wasn't the issue—they had four houses. And they knew I was coming to spend the holidays with them.) So I just kinda sat there and watched them open presents from one another and me. No one said anything about not having gifts for me, they just said thank you and that was that.

"While I know the spirit of the season is to give, not to get, I thought that at least his mother could have wrapped something small up for me so I wouldn't have to sit there awkwardly. (My mom makes it a point that everyone has 'something to open' on Christmas, no matter who comes to spend the holidays with us—I was taught that it's just the polite thing to do.) I was also surprised that my boyfriend didn't say anything to his family members beforehand about how I was making them all gifts, since he watched me work on them for weeks."

WTF? *My ex and his family usually spoke to one another in Croatian, but all of them were also fluent in English. You'd expect that they'd speak English when I went out to dinner or spent holidays with them. Instead, they talked in Croatian, making no attempt at involving me in the conversation, and most of the time they didn't even bother to translate parts so I could somewhat follow. Turned out that they even talked about me in Croatian, blatantly staring and chatting about how terrible I was because I didn't speak their language."*

His family expects too much from you.

Conversely, your man's parents may welcome you a little too warmly and assume you're ready to take on responsibilities that are beyond your years or your level of intimacy with them. If they tell you that you need to contribute money to the family trust or give Great-Grandma Alma her weekly sponge baths, and you're not even engaged to your guy, they're taking advantage of you simply because you happen to be dating their son.

In a less-extreme example, watch out for parents who expect your guy, and therefore you, to be at their beck and call. Maybe they demand you both to drop everything when they decide to come into town unannounced. Or perhaps they mandate that your boyfriend travel to their home every holiday, not respecting the fact that you have parents, too. An über-demanding family will create tension not only in your relationship with your man but also in your bond with your own family as you constantly cater to your guy's family and give your own second billing.

If this situation arises, you need to ask your guy to lay down the law with his 'rents. If he's not willing to tell his relatives to simmer down, especially when it comes to splitting time between your families, or responds with something like "That's just how my family is," he's not ready to prioritize your needs before his mom and dad's—a red flag that he's not really ready for an adult relationship. Inform him that this is going to have to change if he wants you to be a part of his life.

BIG RED-FLAG STORY:

"When I was young I dated this guy for three years. It got fairly serious and we decided to take our relationship to the next level and move in together. During the move, he and one of his sisters sat me down and told me that if we moved in together, we were essentially married and that it was time I started 'pulling my weight.' I had no clue what 'weight' they were referring to.

"Turned out, he had a sister in her forties with severe disabilities, who was soon going to be turned over to our care. His parents could no longer care for her and my boyfriend was listed as her power of attorney and next legal guardian. Being in my early

20s, I was in no way prepared or eager to be a full-time care-giver. It would have been nice to know all of this before I paid for the moving van and moved all my stuff. After the lease was up, I decided our relationship was, too."

THE BOTTOM LINE:

As you get to know your guy's family members better, and your relationship becomes more serious, be sure you can respond to the following questions—and that you like the answers: Who are these people, really? What do they value?

More importantly, what do they expect from you? If they go to church every Sunday, they are likely to want their grandchildren (your kids) to do so as well. On the other hand, if they're atheists, they may end up having a problem with you Bar Mitzvah-ing your son (even if he has an awesome Bar Mitzvah theme). Work this stuff out before things get too serious or you're bound to be stuck belonging to a family that either won't accept you for who you are or assumes you're planning to adapt to their ways.

Aside from the red flags mentioned in this chapter, also look for some of the big warning signs that your guy's family just might not be the type you'd want to join for the long haul—for instance, if his relatives are full-on verbally abusive toward one another or if they continually make racist or sexist jokes (we're a bit judgmental of that kind of behavior, sorry). Another warning sign to consider is if any members of your guy's immediate family have significant personality-altering medical conditions like alcoholism or bipolar disorder that are being left untreated.

Sure, this is heavy stuff—but that's why we're mentioning it. While these red flags might not be reasons to break up with your guy, they're issues that you'll need to assess not just for you, but for your future brood o' babes.

TOP TEN RED FLAGS:
What He Does During Dinner With Your Parents

1. Kisses your entire family "hello"—on the lips
2. Asks everyone to eat more quickly so he can catch the start of the Lakers game
3. Burps then blows it in your dad's face
4. Gets sauced then tries for some tableside PDA
5. Suggests you put back that second dinner roll
6. Tells your mom she has "nice knockers"
7. Gets your underage brother drunk
8. Picks food out of his teeth at the table
9. Flirts with the waitress
10. Orders the most expensive menu item then barely eats it

He's the Worst by Association

You can tell a lot about a person by the company he or she chooses to keep. If your man marches to the beat of his friends' drums—and they're playing a ridiculous, offensive, or outdated song—we say you're better off finding another bandleader.

> *Red-Flag Rule #44:* It pretty much goes without saying that a guy who has less-than-stellar friends is most likely less-than-stellar himself.

Sure, your boyfriend may not be just like his friends, but if he's spending a lot of time with a particular person or affiliation, it's fair to assume that he values the characteristics they possess. So, when his friends are neo-Nazis and he's heading off to KKK meetings "just to see what they're like," you may want to question his judgment. Even if he doesn't directly express the opinions or beliefs of these people to you, he obviously isn't picky about who he spends his time with.

When the man of your dreams has a nightmarish crew, it's time for you to evaluate how your man's friends and associations will ultimately affect your relationship with him.

His friends are terrible.

Immature, disloyal, bigoted . . . there are a number of ways in which people can suck. Even though many men can get along with just about anybody, they often choose close friends with similar interests and opinions. So, although he may act dreamy when you're alone together, he may alter for the worse in the presence of his terrible troops. Even if he doesn't morph into a monster in his homies' presence, the fact that he sits back and laughs at their asshole tendencies shows that he doesn't have strong morals or the wherewithal to stand behind them.

Also watch out for the successful guy with deadbeat friends: If his pals are unemployed druggies with criminal histories, it's very possible that he'll end up an accomplice. And if you happen to be hanging with his loser crew when they're doing something shady, you could find yourself behind bars trying to explain to the cops that you had nothing to do with the cocaine his friends were snorting in your apartment.

Telling your guy that his friends stink and that he should ditch them is not the way to go about solving this situation—he'll likely get offended and defensive when you question the value of his friendships, especially if they are long-standing ones. Before you go writing all his pals off as losers, ask your man exactly what he values about each of them: You could be surprised to learn that his jerky friend once drove four hours in the middle of the night to pick him up when his car broke down—forty miles away, proving his loyalty.

But if he has nothing redeeming to say about any of his pals, you should probably reassess what's redeeming about him and decide if the relationship is worth continuing.

BIG RED-FLAG STORY:

"My ex and his friends got into a ton of physical fights over the stupidest crap: For example, they'd flip out if someone at a bar said hi to one of their girlfriends or made a sarcastic remark at their expense. Though I never actually witnessed one of these fights or even saw him get particularly angry, the fact that he'd join his buddies in punching people for no good reason should have given me an idea of how immature he was."

His ex-girlfriends are crazy.

A man with endless stories about depressed, suicidal, or abusive exes either turns normal gals loony or likes loony girls because he enjoys the drama, needs to feel superior, or thinks he can save them. He'll probably either make mountains of your molehills—by constantly trying to rile you up—or drop you the second he gets bored. God forbid you're emotionally stable.

BIG RED-FLAG STORY:

"When my boyfriend told me he had a history of dating mentally ill women, I thought this was mere coincidence. Over the course of the relationship, it became apparent that he liked girls with problems because they made him feel normal and better about himself. This is not speculation—he broke up with me because I 'wasn't crazy enough' and made him feel like he had issues. Obviously, he did have issues."

Don't let a guy drive you crazy with his taste for insanity. When you're the only sane girlfriend in a line of cuckoos, you may want to question both his judgment and treatment of women.

His group associations are questionable.

Clearly, a guy who joins extremist movements, belongs to a gang, or participates in a "fight club" is either as insane as the people he interacts with or completely desperate for approval. His willingness to adopt the creeds of anyone who'll preach to him shows that he has no sense of self. And if he changes affiliations more than you change your outfit before going out, he won't offer you very much stability.

A dude who genuinely feels strongly attracted to the beliefs of an immoral organization is almost certainly black at the core and will likely try to bring you to the dark side with him. However, your man's devotion to other groups and associations that are not destructive or built on prejudice may also be questionable. If a guy is paying dues in order to have friends, or spends a lot of time volunteering only to brag about what a good person he is, his behavior may reflect the kind of guy he is and change your opinion of him.

BIG RED-FLAG STORY:

"I briefly dated a guy who told me that he was a part of this social club in Los Angeles called 'The Bachelors,' which is basically a glorified fraternity for single men over 25 so they don't feel like total losers for not being able to get laid. The group holds antiquated events called 'Stag Dinners' and 'The Bachelor Ball' and frequently has mixers with its female equivalent, called 'The Spinsters.' Of course, the guy was just as pretentious and douche-y as the group he belonged to."

He's the anti-you.

Sure, opposites attract, but complete opposites repel (science confirms this). While it may be intriguing and exciting to date your counterself, a guy with ideologies on the other end of the spectrum from yours won't work out. He may not be a bad guy, but his core values are too different for your union to last long-term.

BIG RED-FLAG STORY:

"My friends set me up with a guy. Going into the date I had a feeling it wouldn't work out because I'm a free-spirited liberal and I knew he was a tightwad conservative. While I enjoyed his company and didn't dislike him, this dichotomy ruled nearly every conversation we had. By the end of the night, I was completely exhausted from having to argue my case for everything, from why I believe in astrology to why I don't want to be a housewife. I couldn't imagine mustering the energy for date number two, let alone an actual relationship."

Ultimately, this kind of man is the worst . . . for you, anyway. If you're a practicing Christian, probably not a good idea to date an outspoken atheist; if you work at an environmental nonprofit, you may have difficulties dating a big oil exec. Enough said.

THE BOTTOM LINE:

When you date a guy, you also date his pals, past, and pastimes—like his family, these are extensions of him. While you don't have to get along with all of your guys' friends or support all of his activities, if his choices almost always initiate a gag reflex, it's a good sign that your pairing is not meant to be.

A guy who chooses to associate with everyone from rejects to racists obviously isn't a good judge of character and can't be trusted to make other decisions, specifically those pertaining to you and your relationship with him. Since the lens through which you see the world is a totally different prescription than his, you may not be able to come to clear conclusions when you encounter obstacles along the relationship road. So either learn to live with his ideologies or find a guy whose associations inspire, rather than nauseate, you.

TOP TEN RED FLAGS:
His Tattoo

1. Another woman's name
2. His own name
3. The URL for his blog, *www.fratboy4life.com*
4. A portrait of his kid's face (a reminder to pay child support?)
5. A tribal armband
6. Nipples tattooed on his butt cheeks so they look like boobs
7. Tear drops
8. Eyes on the back of his head
9. The Kool-Aid Man busting through his skin
10. Bull horns on his pubic bone

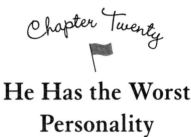

Chapter Twenty

He Has the Worst Personality

So far, this part has covered the various aspects of a man's life that make him the worst: his choice of job (or lack thereof), family, friends, etc. But sometimes the problem is simply the man himself. And since his personality is the foundation upon which he's built, if you think it has a faulty design, recognize that a relationship with him will be rocky.

> *Red-Flag Rule #45:* If a guy tells you he respects you too much to date you, heed his warning. He knows himself better than you do.

Unfortunately, there's not much you can do about a guy with a questionable character or a pitiful personality except hope he changes, and as we know all too well, men are pretty set in their ways by the time we get to them. In fact, any potential personality shift in a guy for the better may take your man years of growing up, getting over himself, or going to therapy—whether or not you want to stick around while he does that is your choice, of course, but we wouldn't advise holding your breath.

From our experience and the multitude of stories we've heard firsthand or received on our blog, the following not-so-awesome traits typically telegraph trouble if you're dating a man afflicted with them. Whether these attributes pop up right away during the dating process or you slowly realize them after you're already in a full-blown relationship, we're certain that they make a dude the absolute worst.

He's pretentious.

Red-Flag Rule #46: If a guy feels the need to tell you that he is not critical, judgmental, or self-righteous, we'd argue there's a million-to-one shot he is.

There are few things more irritating than dating a guy who goes through life convinced he's always right . . . about everything. Combine that with a misguided sense of importance, and you've got one pretentious dude on your hands who's apt to turn up his nose at those who don't follow his "proper" code of conduct. Condescending, self-important, and pompous, this is not the kind of man you want as your life partner.

WTF? *"When my ex paid for something with cash and got change, he would sometimes throw the pennies into the garbage because they were 'annoying.'"*

Natasha once planned a dinner to introduce her friends to her now ex-boyfriend, who happened to be from a very wealthy family. While he (and the friend he brought along) ordered not only full entrees but salads and drinks as well, she and her friends shared a couple of appetizers and drank water (they were in college, money was a bit tight). When the check came, her boyfriend suggested that everyone just split the bill evenly. Not wanting to make her friends fund her guy's (and his friend's) meals, she told him that they should only have to pay for what they ordered. He then said to his friend, loudly, "Well, I guess we're just from another world." (Meaning, of course, the world of money and privilege, in which Natasha and her friends did not reside.)

Pretentious men typically don't understand other people's "worlds," including yours, and they're generally incapable of putting themselves in someone else's shoes. Don't expect this kind of guy to understand, or even listen to, your take on any given situation. His behavior is likely so engrained that he won't even realize he's being insensitive.

BIG RED-FLAG STORY:

"My boyfriend's parents were super-rich and they would often fly us first class to visit them, sometimes even on private planes. While this was really nice of them and all, I did not enjoy my guy's complaints when my parents flew us coach, to Italy, so we could go on a week-long cruise for my graduation that they completely paid for."

Whether he's always focused on brand names, scoffs at your less-literary magazine choices, or insists on using big words (often incorrectly), his superior attitude will result in an inferior relationship. A dude who's constantly concerned with feeling and looking important often ignores the important things in life, like being a good person and boyfriend to you. Whatever the reason your misguided man acts all stuck-up, we suggest you don't put up with his holier-than-thou 'tude.

WTF? *"After not being in touch for a couple of years, I ran into my ex, who proceeded to condescendingly tell me that, because I was not married like him, I couldn't understand the great gift that is marriage or how life-altering holy matrimony is and, therefore, knew nothing about life."*

A WORD ON
Personality Changes

Although scientists previously accepted that a person's personality is fixed by age thirty, recent research from the University of California–Berkeley suggests that most people's personalities actually do change over time. One specific trait the team studied was agreeableness: being warm, generous, and helpful. The study showed that people can become more agreeable starting in their thirties and continuing into their sixties. So there is indeed hope if you're dating a pretentious, rude, narcissistic, or otherwise self-centered dude, but keep in mind that any guy who's an extreme case probably won't change enough to justify waiting around for his about-face.

He's high-maintenance.

There are few things more befuddling to men than how women can spend hours in front of the mirror preening and hundreds of dollars a month on their beauty regimens. (We're not so sure why they mind so much when a lot of our "maintenance" is to look nice for them, but we digress.) But we kind of get it: Girls who need to look perfect at all times tend to be the breed who wrinkle their noses at the thought of drinking beer and eating a hot dog while sitting in the cheap seats. They aren't apt to go camping or stay in a budget hotel. And that hoity-toity attitude can get pretty annoying.

However, this concept works both ways—in fact, we think that high-maintenance men are even worse than their female counterparts. Call us old-fashioned, but there's just something so not sexy about a guy who badgers a waiter to make sure the dressing on his endive salad is in fact fat free or refuses to sleep in sheets with less than a 400-thread count. Jesus H. Christ, be a man.

A guy who spends a ton of money on his moisturizing regime or needs you to analyze his sideburn length every time he shaves will drain your time and patience. Even if you can laugh at his antics, or find them endearing, this fussy fella is surely hard to please, so don't be surprised if he complains when his expectations for you or the relationship aren't met. Generally self-centered, the danger in a high-maintenance man is that everything will always be about him and you'll be expected to play caretaker, cheerleader, and couch doctor. Your needs will be secondary, and you may start to feel neglected. When this becomes the case, stop enabling your man and realize your first responsibility should be to your own emotions.

BIG RED-FLAG STORY:

"I was super excited when I sat down next to a hottie on a cross-country plane flight. (I'd always fantasized about meeting a guy in the air.) Before we took off, he asked the flight attendant for a blanket, which she immediately brought. He opened it, felt it, pressed the button for her to come back, then complained about the quality of the blanket for five uncomfortable minutes. Didn't she know the difference between 100 percent cotton and 60 percent cotton/40 percent polyester? As we were de-boarding, he stopped to speak with the captain about, you guessed it, the stupid blanket."

He's rude.

Like an immature dude, a man who's just plain rude is apt to be an embarrassment to you by association. However, a guy who acts like a child with no manners is far worse than a man who acts like a grown-up with no manners: While the latter guy's behavior can be chalked up to stunted emotional growth, the former dude doesn't really have an excuse . . . he's just an asshole.

A rude man is somewhat similar to a pretentious one in that, when you try to call out his bad behavior, he's apt to vehemently defend why he was entitled to a seat on the subway instead of giving it to an old lady ("My feet hurt."). Having to explain to your guy over and over why what he said or did was wrong gets a little tiring, especially when he's most likely just going to argue with you about it.

And if your dude is indeed rude, start paying attention to who he's rude to: Does he have a problem with authority? Does he reserve his snide remarks for people in the service industry? Or is he an equal-opportunity offender? Which brings us to how he treats you. That's right . . . don't forget that his disrespectful attitude will likely extend to you as well. No. Thanks.

WTF? *"I met a guy online and we scheduled a date. Beforehand he sent me an e-mail saying he wanted to sneak into the coffee shop we were planning on meeting at so he could check me out and make sure I was 'good looking enough.'"*

A guy who can't follow the most basic axiom of all—the golden rule—lives in a world where he's king. Knock him off his throne by letting him know how inappropriate his behavior is. If he's not mature enough to recognize his rudeness and work to alter his attitude, or is aware he's an ass and simply doesn't care, you're officially

dating a dick. He's classless, tactless, and—if you're smart—soon-
to-be girlfriend-less.

BIG RED-FLAG STORY:

"One afternoon, my boyfriend and I were in a designer store,
where he was determined to buy this white suit. I was a little
concerned that he was willing to pay around $800 to look like
the ice cream man, and told him I didn't think white was such a
good color. The salesman at the store agreed with me and tried
to talk my boyfriend into getting the same suit in black or navy.

"If it were me in the situation, and a salesman, a guy whose
job it was to know what looked good on whom, told me I looked
ridiculous in an item of clothing, I hope I would be grateful, or
at least polite. Instead, my boyfriend called me stupid, and then
got into a full-on argument with the salesman, showing his true
colors by pretty much patronizing him. (Saying things like, 'Isn't
it your job to get me to buy stuff from this store?') He ended up
buying a black suit (which he looked great in) but we had our
first fight during the car ride home when I pointed out that he
acted like a jerk."

He's a narcissist.

Red-Flag Rule #47: If a dude's license plate displays the
nickname he gave himself, he's a narcissist.

Luckily, it's not hard to spot a narcissist. They're the ones who come
up to you in the bar, as if they're doing you a favor by talking to you,
hand you their business cards, and say something completely asi-
nine like "Now, when you go home and Google me you're going to

find out I'm an actor, but I'm also a high-powered executive so why don't you check my profile on LinkedIn while you're at it." (Yes, that exact sentence was delivered to Meagan one night by a man who introduced himself as "Handsome.")

While a little self-love is healthy, a man who is too busy gazing lovingly at his own reflection to attend to your needs, or even compliment you once in a while, is not one worth dating. Narcissism is an actual psychological condition that usually requires therapy to remedy. However, in order for treatment to work, the man must be able to admit that he has a personality flaw. Good luck convincing a narcissist that he's anything but perfect. No one, including you, will ever be good enough for him or worth his attention because, after all, he's already found the best lover . . . himself. And when your Romeo is living in his own little world, a healthy relationship is a fantasy.

BIG RED-FLAG STORY:
"I was dating a guy when one night he said he had a big secret to share, something that he had never told anyone before. Sometimes, when he felt too lazy to go out or whatever, he'd take a picture of himself with his camera phone and then look at it in order to remind himself what a good-looking guy he was and how he shouldn't be wasting time lounging inside on the couch."

He's insecure.

Insecure men may be really hung up on their faults, but they are often just as self-absorbed as those narcissists. When you're dating Mr. Insecurity, know that he'll need your constant praise and attention—his ego depends on you to feed his self-confidence.

Natasha was lucky enough to date a guy who always changed in the closet, with the door closed, and stealthily slid in and out of bed to ensure she never really actually caught a glimpse of his member. Maybe he was wildly insecure, or maybe he had a detachable penis, as one of our readers suggested in the comments section of our blog (or perhaps he was insecure about said detachable penis). No matter, his behavior was actually rather sad, and she would have been better off letting the guy work through his body issues solo.

WTF? *"My close male friend was trying to be nice and introduce me to his college buddies, figuring I'd enjoy hanging out with them. Well, one of the dudes became slightly obsessed with talking to me. After giving him my number (and that was it), I started receiving multiple calls and texts a day. Rarely did I pick up or call back, and I nicely tried to explain to the guy that his persistence was a bit much considering we hadn't even been out on a date. A few weeks later, he called me crying, saying he couldn't decide if he wanted to date me or not, as if the ball was in his court."*

> *Red-Flag Rule #48:* The only thing more annoying than a chick who constantly asks if you think she looks fat is a man who constantly asks if you think he looks fat.

Perhaps he was bullied as a kid, cheated on by his last girlfriend, or feels inadequate and emasculated next to a confident woman. Regardless, like the high-maintenance guys, insecure dudes need to man up a bit. We're not saying that men aren't allowed to be self-conscious or have feelings of doubt (after all, we all do), but guys like these need a reality check that the world doesn't in fact revolve around them and their little pity parties.

And forget about ever pointing out an insecure guy's faults— such behavior is likely to get you a nice little tongue-lashing. We know a guy who was so insecure that he would get angry with his girlfriend when she'd tell him that he had something stuck in his teeth. Even though she was nice and as subtle as possible about letting him know, he would demand she never tell him anything of the sort again. Imagine if she were to bring up a real criticism of his behavior toward her—we'd guess he wouldn't be very keen on hearing her out.

We don't advise being in a relationship with an insecure man because guys with ego issues are the same ones who most typically become controlling or abusive. He'll want to keep you on a short leash because he's scared that, if free to roam, you'll find a better boyfriend. Reassuring and complimenting this guy won't always do the trick, either, because everything you say will be turned around and interpreted as a fault on his part.

BIG RED-FLAG STORY:
"After my divorce I decided to go home with a man I met at a bar. He was very tall (6 foot 8), a volleyball player, and quite good-looking. One thing led to another and we eventually tried to have sex. Tried is the key word here. His little guy was unfortunately small (think pinkie finger here, ladies), and it just didn't work out. The (no) sex was followed by two hours of him crying (and still staying the night at my place), more crying in the morning, and repeated texts over the next two months asking me to 'let him try again.'"

He's a busboy.

No, we're not talking about the profession here but rather a personality type that's inspired by it: In restaurants, a busboy is someone who doesn't bring anything to the table, he only takes things away.

A busboy in life does the same thing except he isn't taking away your empty dishes, but rather your credibility when you bring this milquetoast mate out to meet your family and friends.

While there are many forms a busboy can take, the one we most often hear about is the kind of guy who is so agreeable that you're not sure if he's ever expressed his own point of view. The common refrain you'll tell yourself about this guy is "But he's so nice . . . ." However, there's a big difference between being easygoing and being complacent. A guy who's always out to please will treat you well but he'll offer you no challenge or opinion, making him more of a pet than a partner.

BIG RED-FLAG STORY:

"My ex liked my car. He liked my clothes. He liked my cousin's dog. Hell, he liked the massive zit on my nose, as long as I liked it. Questions like 'Do *you* like this movie?' would be met with a brief pause, then a response of 'Do you like this movie?,' a thread that continued from sunup to sundown. If I liked it, he did. If I didn't like it, he didn't. He had no personality of his own. Fun for a little while, I would intentionally trip him up for good measure and then catch him on his slip-up, which would not only elicit a red face, but a really healthy dose of infantile sulking, followed by him bending down to kiss my feet once again."

We all like a guy who will go with the flow, but if he's simply riding the lazy river through your relationship and not expressing any opinions of his own, you're best off canoeing solo. As one of our blog submitters wrote: "It's boring as all hell to have someone acquiesce no matter what . . . unless you've always wanted to be followed around by a mime." Well said, sister.

He's a whiner.

Your boyfriend hates his job, can't stand his boss, works long hours, never gets to go to the gym, is continually stressed, doesn't get the recognition he deserves—and he never shuts up about it. It's not that his life's so terrible; he just complains about everything from having to do his laundry to meeting that last-minute deadline, which makes him the worst to be around.

If his life really does suck, he should do something about it and stop whining. You certainly don't have to subject yourself to his misery. Unless, of course, you're miserable yourself and enjoy his company.

BIG RED-FLAG STORY:

"All my ex wanted to talk about was the many hardships he'd encountered, which weren't really afflictions at all but normal life stuff we've probably all experienced. It might be helpful to explain that he was one of those hipster/emo-types, which I didn't realize when we first met, but no matter if he was emo or messed-up or whatever, constantly talking about how shitty his life was proved to be a major turn-off."

He's just stupid.

While heart is more important than brains, if conversations with your guy make you feel like you're talking not just to a wall but to a white, artless one that makes you want to stab yourself in the eye, you may need to find a man with more than air between his ears.

Sure, this red flag isn't as bad as the others we've just discussed, but supreme stupidity falls under "the worst" because, like dating a busboy, being with a guy who not only has no clue how to treat a woman but also has little to no common sense about life in general can be extremely draining. There's nothing wrong with being "the catch" of the relationship, but come on now, you don't want a guy who's a complete guppy.

Red-Flag Rule #49: Big-headed and small-brained with zero self-awareness—the worst guys are the ones that don't even know how ridiculous they act.

BIG RED-FLAG STORY:

"One guy that I dated could barely spell or read, despite having spent twenty-one years in school. As far as I could tell, none of his teachers covered grammar or even basic math (like addition and subtraction). That said, a positive of him was that he was a great person to call before bed because those conversations literally put me to sleep. He also signed his e-mails with his favorite numbers, which were also his password for everything from his e-mail account to his debit card."

THE BOTTOM LINE:

The reason we bring up the various character-related flags in this part is not to encourage you to develop a judgmental attitude (à la Mr. Pretentious) but instead to show you that these kinds of men really do present problems for the future—as those of us who've dated similar guys already know from experiencing their issues firsthand.

Younger women can be more susceptible to these kinds of "worst" guys, as these men are typically interested in less mature women who haven't had a chance to date around. One of our blog readers sent us a story about a guy she knew who explained to her why men in their late twenties continue to date girls under twenty-three.

"Older girls already know what they want, and they want to change us," he said. "Girls in their early twenties are too naive to know that what they want isn't us." Whether they are emotionally stunted or just plain clueless, men who prey on women who are too inexperienced to know better are, simply, the worst: the worst friends, the worst boyfriends, and the worst lovers.

> *Red-Flag Rule #50:* If your guy turns out to be "the worst," don't be discouraged. Dating is a process of learning what works for you. The good thing about finding men you don't like is that it narrows down who you ultimately do like.

TOP TEN RED FLAGS:
Things He Complains About

1. His imperfect facial symmetry
2. Wearing a condom
3. His six-figure salary
4. The new XBox controllers
5. How unfair God is
6. Not being appreciated by the world
7. His tummy ache
8. Minorities stealing his opportunities
9. The community service he has to do for his DUI
10. The size of his cubicle

WHETHER YOUR GUY is the worst because of his life circumstances, his past, the people and ideologies he associates himself with, or his personality, it's safe to say that these factors will not just affect your opinion of him but will dictate whether or not a long-term partnership between you two is possible.

It's up to you to recognize your brand of "worst" so you can determine for yourself what you can and cannot tolerate. Some girls would be totally cool with the fact that their guy served time in jail but wouldn't be able to handle one whose family made them feel left out. Others would be okay dating a somewhat insecure man but couldn't deal with a dude whose friends were total douchebags. So recognize when your chap's qualities make you queasy and move on early on, knowing that you're one step closer to finding "the one."

Red-Flag Case Study #5

See how many red flags you can spot in just one story:

I went on a date with someone I met online that went like this. Within the first few minutes he: paid for two beers with a one-hundred-dollar bill just to show off the money, rapidly inhaled a pizza and then loudly belched without an apology but rather a "Why are you looking at me like that? I haven't eaten since breakfast and I'm hungry . . . you're not gonna be one of those girls who gets mad because I burped on our first date, are you?", and told me that my earrings

were nice but so big that they distracted from my face.🚩
Then I asked about his family. He said something about
leaving home in his late teens to drive a van around the country and drop acid at various concerts.🚩 And then I asked
what his parents thought about that and he responded with,
"Listen. I really don't want to talk about my parents. Okay?
Will you just drop it?"🚩 That outburst was followed pretty
much immediately by "You're cute. Do you want to make
out?"🚩 I didn't, but booze got the better of me when we left
the bar and I ended up kissing him on the street.

Once I'd broken things off (a good two weeks later . . .
what was I thinking?), he left me an voicemail message that
I kept on my phone and hope to one day play for the world,
so everyone will know what ignoring red flags will lead to.🚩

🚩 He's a douchebag.

🚩 He's clearly not trying to impress or woo her here.

🚩 He's guilting her for having expectations. Yeah, "one of those
girls" who appreciates manners? A gal shouldn't be ashamed of
having (quite normal) standards.

🚩 He thinks *The Game* is a field guide for picking up women.
Newsflash: Offending or being mean to us doesn't actually work.

🚩 He may have a shady past. Something to keep in mind.

🚩 He's got family issues. If a guy won't talk about his parents, that's odd.

🚩 He just wants to get some . . . and he's not smooth in trying to
make it happen.

🚩 He's either creepy, awkward, inappropriately sexual, or *all* of
those things.

Conclusion

The Big Bottom Line

So, we've given you all these warning signs that you should have on your radar as you date, commit to, and maybe even marry a dude. Okay, that's great. Now what?

What all these red flags boil down to is one thing: awareness. When we began collecting red-flag stories, and thinking back to our experiences with the guys who committed them, we realized the importance of simply recognizing the offenses in question. Some red flags are just good to know, others warrant discussions, and some are total dealbreakers. But if you don't have any awareness, or know what to look for, you'll never be able to evaluate these warning signs.

Because we've been in red-flag situations ourselves—and know that even men with good hearts and the best intentions make mistakes—we don't encourage you to outright reject a guy or break up with your boyfriend if he exhibits a couple of episodes of bad behavior. Instead, we're hoping you'll put down this book with a better understanding of what the bigger relationship flags are for you. Only you know what you can or can't accept, and what you will or won't tolerate. This distinction may change a bit as you get older: Surely the type of guy you were attracted to in college—and the behavior you were okay with—won't be the same as the one you're looking for when you're working a steady job and aren't partying three to four nights a week.

What we're asking you to do now with your red-flag awareness is simply this: Really notice how a guy treats you. Then—and this might sound crazy—don't run to your girlfriends for interpretation right away if he does something kind of weird. Instead, think about how your boy's behavior made you feel and ask him to explain his conduct. If you're just dating him, note how he reacts. Is he defensive? Is he more concerned about being right, or about the way you feel? Better to get this stuff out of the way early instead of letting issues fester, or wasting your time on a dude who's just not going to cut it for you in the long run.

If you're in a serious relationship, pay attention to how you both handle the situation in the days and weeks that follow your discussion. When you both can recognize, work through, and develop a plan to fix your problems, your bond will become stronger. Sharing and repairing concerns, red flag or otherwise, is that "work" part people refer to when they imply that relationships are not just jellybeans and sunshine.

Over the course of a relationship both you and your man will make mistakes, hurt each other's feelings, and say things you shouldn't have, committing borderline or full-on flags. No guy is perfect. No person is perfect. So keep in mind that you also need to be conscious of your behavior, taking into consideration how you might be making your man feel, because love is a two-way street. Regardless of who transgresses, the true strength of a relationship lies in how you handle and learn from the offense.

The flip side to this whole awareness thing is that, as you start pondering your partnership, you may realize that you aren't all that pleased. When you examine your guy's actions, you might find that he's treating you poorly or he's not the catch you once thought he was. You may even discover that the issues you two have can't actually be worked through.

Many women hesitate to express their true feelings when they're unhappy in a relationship. We often feel like we "should" be with a person or that we're stuck with him because our parents want us to be with him, we've been together so long already, whatever. Fact is, if it's not right, it's not right—you only live once, so why waste your precious time on a dude you know is not a match? Don't focus on what other people think, impose crazy expectations on yourself, or follow some outdated idea that you need to work things out no matter how terrible the guy is. After all, what about being happy?

Since you're the one in the relationship, seeing your situation objectively is nearly impossible. So here's a tip that we swear by, and we can vouch for this simple suggestion's effectiveness: Make yourself a list of what you want. Natasha does this by dividing a page from her diary down the middle and putting "Yes" and "No" at the top of each column. Meagan draws a circle, putting characteristics she likes on the inside and those she doesn't fancy outside of it. (Julie found her man in college when she was too drunk to think about any of this stuff.)

Using the flags in this book and your dating experience, start noting the qualities you would really want in a guy and the ones you will not stand for. Don't include superficial stuff like "must look like a young Paul Newman" or "can't be shorter than six feet" but real issues like "can't be best friends with his ex" or "actually needs to refer to me as his girlfriend."

If you can't think of any yeses or nos right now, that's okay—just jot things down as they come to you. Reflect on past relationships, not to determine how much of an asshole your ex-boyfriend was, but to help clarify exactly what worked for you and what didn't, as well as what was missing. The lists don't need to be long—maybe five to ten points each. Hopefully they'll help you remember your standards when your relationship circumstances get a tad dismal. We all deserve a bodacious beau, but we'll never get one if we don't stick to our guns.

The reason we tell you to include both positive and not-so-positive qualities is because, while this book talks solely about the red-flag warning signs, that doesn't mean you should simply focus on only the bad qualities of your boyfriend or a potential one. While dating or being committed isn't all lovey-dovey all the time, give reward where it's due and appreciate your guy if you've found a good one. (You could even call a man's positive qualities "green lights," if you feel so inclined.)

Despite what you may think or what you've experienced in your dating life so far, there are a lot of these great, green-light-illuminating men out there. For some reason, we seem to go for the not-so-good ones first. But, as cartoonist Mort Walker so aptly said, nice guys don't finish last, they win before the game even starts. Rounding the bases with jerks only leaves you jaded: Once you commit to dating guys who treat you how you want—and deserve—to be treated, your green-light guy will be waiting for you at home plate.

Red-Flag Rules

Red-Flag Rule #1: If you're not sure whether or not you're a guy's girlfriend, you probably aren't.

Red-Flag Rule #2: If he still claims to be "Single" on Facebook or hasn't deleted his Match.com profile, he's still actively looking for a girlfriend, which you apparently are not.

Red-Flag Rule #3: If you ask the guy you've been sleeping with where he sees the relationship going, and he replies, "I don't want us to be anything more than this," no matter how great the sex is, don't expect a commitment anytime soon.

Red-Flag Rule #4: If he's hinting at not just a goodnight kiss, but a till-the-morning romp ten minutes into your first date, we guarantee he's looking for a bedmate, not a soul mate.

Red-Flag Rule #5: If your "dates" with a guy consist solely of booze and booty calls, chances are he's not your boyfriend.

Red-Flag Rule #6: If he tells you he's got a "busy day" the moment his alarm goes off, don't expect him to take you to breakfast.

Red-Flag Rule #7: If a guy declares his love for you, and he's currently dating your best friend—run.

Red-Flag Rule #8: If he explicitly says, "I'm never going to be the boyfriend type," take his word for it and find a more loyal lad.

Red-Flag Rule #9: If he's overly eager to engage in gay culture, he may also be overly eager to engage in gay coitus.

Red-Flag Rule #10: If a guy can't hear the word "vagina" without giggling, he should not be permitted to touch yours.

Red-Flag Rule #11: A guy who's not man enough to have your back on all occasions, even if it means upsetting his mother, isn't worth keeping around.

Red-Flag Rule #12: If a guy can pick up a phone and send you a text, surely he can use the same phone and call you with it.

Red-Flag Rule #13: If you're always the one doing all the sharing, it's time your man opens up and starts telling you something more substantial than the score of the game.

Red-Flag Rule #14: If there's mold growing in your guy's fridge, you should probably check the date on his condoms.

Red-Flag Rule #15: If your boyfriend has acquired more than $385 in overdraft fees—in the span of two days—you probably don't want to combine your finances.

Red-Flag Rule #16: If a guy has to ask how many times you came, chances are you didn't.

Red-Flag Rule #17: If he mashes your lady parts like he's kneading pizza dough, tell him to lighten up before you're too swollen to cross your legs.

Red-Flag Rule #18: A man should never use the word "pussy" while he's in yours.

Red-Flag Rule #19: If a guy turns you for doggie style within the first couple of times you sleep together, don't be surprised when he tries to stick it in your ass soon after.

Red-Flag Rule #20: A guy should never whip out his ex-girlfriend's vibrator to use on you. There are just some things that should be purchased anew.

Red-Flag Rule #21: A guy should never say, "It's all in your head" when you tell him that you need to stop during sex because it hurts.

Red-Flag Rule #22: If he accuses you of being "sexually repressed" when you tell him that joking about rape isn't funny, he probably doesn't abide by the "no means no" rule.

Red-Flag Rule #23: When your boyfriend agrees not to break up with you as long as you consent to anal sex, where does his guilting stop?

Red-Flag Rule #24: If a guy doesn't even *reach* for a condom the first time you have sex, he doesn't respect you or your body.

Red-Flag Rule #25: If he's inconsiderate or insensitive during the so-called honeymoon phase, he's not going to suddenly start treating you better once the excitement and newness of the relationship wear off.

Red-Flag Rule #26: It's better to have loved and lost than to be stuck in a relationship that's no longer full of love at all.

Red-Flag Rule #27: If your guy can't tolerate your quirks now, he's only going to resent them—and you—later.

Red-Flag Rule #28: If the guy you're dating is friends with all the girls he used to sleep with—and also expects to be friends with you, should you break up—he's delusional.

Red-Flag Rule #29: If you have to think twice about whether or not your man is treating you right, you're already thinking too hard.

Red-Flag Rule #30: If your boyfriend only talks about marrying you when he's drunk, you probably shouldn't start planning your bridal registry.

Red-Flag Rule #31: If you find out your guy has never said "I love you," even though he previously dated another girl seriously for years, this information could signal intimacy issues.

Red-Flag Rule #32: If a guy tells you "I wish we'd met each other later in life" . . . he means he still wants time to sow his wild oats, not settle down.

Red-Flag Rule #33: If your man's got marriage—to you—on the brain, he'll eventually start speaking in we's. If he says "when I get married" rather than "when we get married," he's not thinking about anything long term . . . with you, anyway.

Red-Flag Rule #34: If some dude tells you on a first date that you'll make a great mom to his kids, he's not looking for a partner to share the rest of his life with, he's looking for a babysitter.

Red-Flag Rule #35: If your vibrator is consistently serving as designated hitter, your man may be rounding the bases with another player, if you know what we mean.

Red-Flag Rule #36: If right after you sleep with him, a guy tells you he feels guilty for having sex with you because he feels like he just cheated on his ex, put your clothes back on.

Red-Flag Rule #37: If a guy you're dating knows, to the day, how long he's been broken up with his ex, he's still in love with her.

Red-Flag Rule #38: If your alleged knight in shining armor swoops in offering to improve every area of your life, he'll probably end up trying to control your life. Make sure he treats you like a princess, not like a project.

Red-Flag Rule #39: If your boyfriend tells you that you've changed since starting therapy, and he would like you to stop going, what he really means is that you've started standing up for yourself, and he would like you to stop.

Red-Flag Rule #40: If he's not just taking the reins, but strangling you with them, knock him off his high horse before your heart gets trampled.

Red-Flag Rule #41: If the guy you're dating tells you he can't commit to a relationship right now because he's "processing a lot," don't wait around for him to work through his shit. We're *all* processing a lot . . . it's called life.

Red-Flag Rule #42: If the family tree is rotten, the apple that falls from it will be, too: Your guy's relatives' behavior and interactions reveal who he really is and explain how he got that way.

Red-Flag Rule #43: If a guy treats his mother like dirt, it's very likely he'll treat you terribly, too.

Red-Flag Rule #44: It pretty much goes without saying that a guy who has less-than-stellar friends is most likely less-than-stellar himself.

Red-Flag Rule #45: If a guy tells you he respects you too much to date you, heed his warning. He knows himself better than you do.

Red-Flag Rule #46: If a guy feels the need to tell you that he is not critical, judgmental, or self-righteous, we'd argue there's a million-to-one shot he is.

Red-Flag Rule #47: If a dude's license plate displays the nickname he gave himself, he's a narcissist.

Red-Flag Rule #48: The only thing more annoying than a chick who constantly asks if you think she looks fat is a man who constantly asks if you think he looks fat.

Red-Flag Rule #49: Big-headed and small-brained with zero self-awareness—the worst guys are the ones that don't even know how ridiculous they act.

Red-Flag Rule #50: If your guy turns out to be "the worst," don't be discouraged. Dating is a process of learning what works for you. The good thing about finding men you don't like is that it narrows down who you ultimately do like.

About the Authors

Natasha Burton is the Relationships Editor of *Glo*, a women's website partnered with MSN.com. Her work has appeared in *People*, *Glamour*, WomansDay.com, FHMOnline, and Outblush.com. When she's not grilling her friends about the most intimate details of their love lives, she's most likely in the kitchen whipping up some Italian food.

Julie Fishman is a humor writer who works in screen, print, and web. She currently teaches at a college in Hollywood, pens a weekly cocktail column for *Glo* called "Hump Day Happy Hour," and dreams up irreverent sitcom ideas. Aside from writing, she's either hanging with her pooch and drinking wine, or talking about hanging with her pooch and drinking wine.

Meagan McCrary is an L.A.–based yoga teacher with an adventurous spirit for romance who has written about health and wellness for a variety of local lifestyles magazines. While she spends most of her days teaching Anusara yoga and giving private lessons to her various clients, she finds time to work on "being present" (and her tan) at the beach under the California sun.

Natasha, Julie, and Meagan are all Santa Monica–dwelling Pisceans who met while earning their Master's of Professional Writing degrees at the University of Southern California.